WELCOME

...to the exciting world of painting. Whether you want to paint the walls of your home, try a faux finish or create a silk-painted masterpiece, this book is for you.

If you've always admired watercolors or wanted to dabble with oils, there are instructions and tips to help you get started.

Our goal is to give you information and inspiration. Let this book be your guide to exploring all the different techniques. We hope that you'll try several of them and then concentrate on the one you love the most. Creatively expressing yourself with painting can become a cherished hobby, useful talent or a delightful pastime.

Happy Painting!

C·O·N·T·E·N·T·S

Painting walls is the least-expensive way to make a fantastic decorating statement. Beautifully painted walls set the tone for your home. The right color choice can make your surroundings look bigger or smaller; contemporary, or old-fashioned. Whether you're painting a new home, redecorating, or getting ready to sell, all it takes is a few cans of paint, brushes or rollers, and simple tools. A wide variety of paints exist for any budget or type of project.

It is time to paint when wall surfaces look worn, faded, or chalky, or when you feel your home needs a lift! Don't wait until paint is blistering or cracked.

Three things contribute to the long-lasting appearance of your painted walls - paint quality, surface type, and preparation.

Selecting Paint Colors

Make a decorating plan before you paint. Look carefully through home decorating magazines. Check out model homes and homes of friends. Watch home decorating shows on television. Find a paint store with a computer for viewing different paint color schemes. Assemble a color notebook (see page 7) to take with you as you shop for paints. Add paint chips to the notebook as you visit paint stores.

Paint always looks at least 4 times darker on the wall surface than on the paint chip. Select the sample you like best, then buy a quart that is 3 - 4 times lighter than your choice. Try it on a small

section of the room, then observe its effect during daylight, and evening light. You can always paint over it if you don't like it. This method will save you money in the long run, and you'll be more satisfied with the results.

Before you start, consider the following questions. Should you do the job yourself or hire a professional? Even small jobs can be tricky for first-time painters. Should you select water-based, or oil based paint? Wear and tear on wall surface often dictates paint type.

Paint

Synthetic, water-based paints are odorless, clean up with soap and water, dry faster, are fade resistant and don't become brittle.

Flat paint is the best choice if wall surface is not perfectly smooth. Select satin or semi-gloss for high-wear rooms like the kitchen, bathroom, and children's rooms because its surface withstands frequent cleaning. Semi-gloss reflects light, thus adds drama to small rooms or rooms used at night, such as a dining room. Semi-gloss is most often chosen for woodwork and trim.

Oil-based paint has a strong smell, requires clean-up with mineral spirits, takes the longest time to dry but is more water resistant.

For your best choice - consult a professional. A trusted local paint store is a good source.

Decorating With Color

Colors can make all the difference when decorating a home. Colors can warm lives, lift moods, make you happy, create memories, inspire and comfort you.

When choosing colors, select an existing fabric, carpet, or large piece of furniture in your room. Then match this to a paint chip. This will become the central color in your color scheme.

Then decide what type of color scheme you want:

Bright and contrasty - such as red and green or yellow and purple

Soft and Subdued - shades in the same color family - such as green, medium green, and light green.

Dark and dramatic - deeper tones with black or darker accents.

Then decide the mood you want:
Cheerful - reds, yellows, pinks
Calming - blues, greens, purples
Secure - beiges, shades of white, grays

Then put these all together and come up with your very own color scheme.

To make things even simpler, some paint companies offer whole systems for helping you select colors. Glidden Paint offers a color system which is grouped by moods, such as vibrant, fresh, warm, and calm. Paint cards are available with symbols to distinguish the moods. Decide on the mood you want to achieve, match paint colors to the symbols and come up with a winning combination!

Other paint companies have their own systems. Color catalogs are available with paint chips organized by coordinating color schemes. This takes the guesswork out of choosing colors.

Fresh

Vibrant

no curtains - the view is too pretty!

← drapes

Color Matching computers

Can't find a paint chip in the color you're trying to match? To get exactly the color of paint you want - take a sample from the item you're matching to a paint store that has a color matching computer. The computer reads the color and translates it into a paint formula. They mix the paint while you wait.

If you're not sure how you're going to like a certain color, buy just a pint and test it on your walls in one small spot. Watch the swatch at different times of day to check out its effect under different light conditions. See if it matches your accessories. You might want to try 2 or 3 different pints to make sure which is right. When you've decided, buy the rest of the paint and start painting right over your test swatches.

Inspirational Notebook

Start a notebook. Devote a section to each room in your house. Tape or glue swatches of fabric from draperies, furniture, rugs, wallpaper, etc. Note measurements of the walls. You might want to add pictures of rooms from magazines that you really like. This will make it much easier when you go to the paint store and start collecting paint chips.

Don't be intimidated when it comes to selecting paint colors for your home. Just remember to go with the colors you love and you can't go too far wrong. Also, remember, paint is inexpensive. If you don't like the color you've painted, you can always paint right over it!

Warm

Calm

new shower curtains

P·A·I·N·T·I·N·G

TOOLS AND SUPPLIES

Primer - Some surfaces require primer before final paint is applied. Some examples include dark surfaces which will be painted a light color, worn or rusted surfaces, heavily textured surfaces like brick, masonry and dark wood. Use primer as an inexpensive undercoat when two coats of paint are required.

Surface compound and application tool - Fill cracks, holes, and small uneven areas, then sand smooth for best appearance.

7" to 9" Roller for flat surfaces - (Nylon cover for water-based paint; nylon/wool or lamb's wool cover for oil-based paint.

1" to 2" Angled or Flat brushes - for trim, corners and ceiling lines. (Synthetic fiber or foam for water-based paint; natural bristle for oil-based)

Paint tray and Plastic liners

Roller handle extension for ceilings

Sandpaper, Painter's tape, Edger, Wooden stirrers

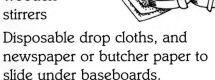

Disposable drop cloths, and newspaper or butcher paper to slide under baseboards.

Ladder

Old clothes, hat, Protective eyewear

How much paint to buy

It's important to buy the correct amount of paint initially because it's difficult to get the exact shade later - especially if you're having the paint mixed at the store.

Here's a formula for figuring how much you'll need:

Measure the width of each wall of the room or rooms you'll be painting. Multiply the perimeter total by the height of the walls.

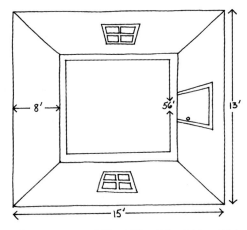

Perimeter: 15'+15'+13'+13'= 56'
One gallon covers approximately 400 square feet.

          perimeter - 56 ft.
          height -   x8 ft.
                      448 sq. ft.

You'll need 2 gallons of paint.

GENERAL PREPARATION

1. Remove draperies, pictures, mirrors, switch plates, hardware.

2. Cover furniture and floor with drop cloths. Cover non-removable light fixtures with newspaper or plastic bags and painter's tape.

Wall Surface Preparation

Wallpapered Walls

Remove old wallpaper. Depending on the paper and adhesive, choices include spray-on chemical or steaming. Rent steamers at rental companies. Sand any glossy spots.

Applying paint over wallpaper is possible if papered surface is very smooth, firm and even. Primer must be applied over paper before painting.

Plaster Walls

Unpainted plaster walls must be cured prior to painting. Treat unpainted plaster walls with a solution of 1 pint household vinegar to 1 gallon of water. Rinse with plain water and let dry before applying primer.

Drywall or Wallboard

Tape panel joints, patch holes, cracks and surface blemishes, sand and prime.

Painted Walls

Previously painted walls may require a variety of clean-up techniques before painting. Wash areas soiled by greasy substances with household detergent or wall cleaner designed to remove greasy residue. For mold and mildew, wash with a solution of 1 quart household bleach and 3 quarts water. Make sure wall surface is dry, and mildew free.

Remove loose paint, patch holes, cracks, and surface blemishes, sand and prime.

APPLYING PAINT

Use the professional painter's techniques to insure great results! Some easy first steps help guarantee success.

1. Precondition roller cover used for synthetic paint, by rinsing in water and spinning dry. (Don't precondition a lamb's-wool roller.)

2. Cover the metal paint tray with a plastic liner to make cleanup simple.

3. Fill tray with one third of paint.

4. Load the roller with paint by rolling it in the deeper end of the tray, then smoothing it on the sloping surface until the paint is distributed evenly.

5. **Paint ceilings first.** If your ceiling color is a different color, use a brush or edging tool to paint around the edges. For touch-ups, use a lightly-loaded roller, or daub with a brush.

6. Use a brush or edging tool to outline corners, baseboards and around window and door frames.

7. **Paint the walls next**, in areas 2 feet square. If you use a roller, roll out the letter M as shown. Then roll over area with parallel strokes to even out texture.

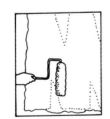

8. **Paint the trim** - use an angled brush. Use painter's tape over areas not freshly painted. Remove tape quickly after painting to avoid pulling the paint away with the tape.

9. **Paint doors and windows -**

Paneled Doors -

a) Cover, or remove hinges, knob and latch with painter's tape. Immediately remove any paint accidentally spilled on hardware.

b) Paint the top panels first.

c) Paint panels by brushing across, then up and down. Paint any remaining areas then paint door edge.

d) Finish by painting frame and jamb.

Sash Windows -

a) Raise inside sash and lower outside sash.

b) Paint inside sash, crossbars, then frame. DO NOT paint top edge of inside sash. That surface is used to move the sash.

c) Paint outside sash crossbars, then frame. DO NOT paint bottom edge of outside sash. Let paint dry completely.

d) Move both sashes down as far as they go. Paint upper part of check rails. Let paint dry.

e) Raise both sashes and paint lower check rails. Let paint dry completely.

f) Move both sashes to center of window. Paint parts of outside sash that were obstructed. Paint top edge of inside sash.

g) Paint window casing, then sill.

Casement Windows -

a) Open window out (or in).

b) Paint top, side, then bottom edge.

c) Paint crossbars, frame, casing, then sill.

CLEAN UP

Proper cleaning of painting tools and accessories extend the value of your investment in these items, and reduce labor time for future painting projects.

1. Clean all brushes and rollers with soap and warm water. Use mineral spirits to clean oil-based paint brushes and rollers. Shape brushes to a neat, flat, pointed edge while still wet. Hang brushes upside-down to air-dry. Remove as much paint as possible from roller cover. Clean roller and handle. Spin roller to restore cover surface nap. Dry roller cover on end.

2. Discard tray liner, or clean tray thoroughly.

3. Keep leftover paint for touch ups. Cover top of open can with plastic wrap, replace lid, tap firmly in place and label can with color and date of use.

ALTERNATE PAINTING METHODS

Spraying - can cut job time in half. To get successful results, this technique takes practice. More preparation is needed because everything must be masked and cleanup is more involved.

Power Rollers - power rollers are also available at rental yards. A power roller forces paint through a tube into the roller. Although there is no tray to clean up, the equipment can be tricky.

P·A·I·N·T·I·N·G

Instructions for four popular faux finishes
(See Chapter Two for more finishes)

Ragging Off
Paint roller and tray
Paint - Latex - 2 different shades
Glaze
Rags - old T-shirts, chamois leather or plastic bags, and protective gloves

1. Apply latex (usually the lighter shade) and let dry overnight. Apply another coat if necessary.

2. Mix the darker shade of paint with the glaze (two parts of paint to two parts of glaze).

3. Apply the glaze to areas of about 4' x 4' and work quickly before glaze dries. Work from the top of wall down. (It helps to work with a partner.)

4. With a crumpled up cloth or plastic bag, dab over the glaze. Repeat this process over the wet glaze replacing the rag or bag with a new one as the old one fills with paint.

5. Apply more glaze to a new area and repeat this process until the wall is finished. Be sure to overlap the new edge to the section you have just done.

Bagging - one shade of paint
Paint roller and tray
Plastic drop sheets or trash bags
Protective gloves
Paint - Latex
Glaze

1. Using roller, paint walls (in color of your choice). Allow to dry overnight.

2. Mix two parts of the paint (color of your choice) to two parts of glaze.

3. Apply glaze using the roller. Work very quickly before glaze mixture dries. Use a partner to help with this process.

4. While glaze is still wet, apply a thin plastic sheet over the wet glaze. If using trash bags, be sure to slit up the sides to give you a larger piece. Using hands, smooth the plastic against the wall and wrinkle, rub and crinkle it. This should take about five minutes. Remove plastic and throw away.

5. Repeat this process using a fresh piece of plastic until the wall is completely finished.

Sponging On

Paint roller and tray
Large sea sponge
Paint tray or foam plate
Protective gloves
1" brush
Paint - Latex (2 or 3 colors)

1. Paint walls with first color of paint (usually the lighter shade). Let dry overnight.

2. Dampen sea sponge with water and wring out. Dip sea sponge into the second shade of paint on a foam plate.   Dab on paper towel to remove some of the paint.

3. Start anywhere on wall. Sponge on second color using a pouncing motion. Fill in missed areas.

4. Reload sponge and continue dabbing wall until sponging is complete.

5. Apply third color if desired. Repeat Step #3.

Corners - cut off 1/3 of a sea sponge to a flat edge. With the straight edge against the wall, sponge the corners starting at top of wall.

For really difficult corners - use a 1" brush and a straight up and down "pouncing" motion.

Bagging - two shades of paint

Paint roller and tray
Plastic drop sheets or trash bags
Protective gloves
Paint - Latex (2 different shades)
Glaze

1. Apply one shade of paint (the lighter shade works best). Allow to dry overnight.

2. Mix the darker shade of paint with the glaze (two parts of paint to two parts of glaze).

3. Then follow the same instructions as "bagging in one shade of paint".

TIPS

•Be sure to try out your paint combination on a practice board before applying to a wall.

•Ragging off and bagging goes faster with two people. One to apply, the other to remove.

F·A·U·X · F·F

Faux, (pronounced "foe") is a type of painting developed centuries ago by the European merchant classes to emulate embellishments and materials found in the great castles of the aristocracy. This type of painting involves transformation, illusion and deception.

Achieving the look of marble, tortoiseshell or precious malachite is a less expensive alternative to the genuine object.

In the following pages, discover several finishes that have transformed ordinary objects into objects d' art.

Create the look of Serpentine Marble - a green stone, veined with white and traces of black. The papier-mache box, clay pot and frame have each been finished in this popular technique. The Parson's table, on which these items are displayed, is also marbleized. (page 21)

Splashed Marble is easy to mimic with just a little paint and a splashing tool. Small projects such as the clock and clay pot are perfect for trying this finish. (page 22)

The hat box, clock, mini jewelry box and frame have all been finished to reproduce the look of tortoiseshell, a glowing combination of brown, ochre and umber. (page 23)

A patina gold finish imitates the look of an old gold or antique finish. Add a soft patina to boxes, clay pots and other surfaces with paint and glaze. (page 25)

Malachite's distinctive turquoise and green banding pattern transforms a frame, hat box and small jewelry box into eye-catching focal points. The pattern is easily achieved using a combing tool over the glaze. (page 25)

The country look of this picket fence shelf (upper left) has been achieved using a color washing technique. The natural pattern of the wood shows through and is given a subtle, aged finish by using diluted paints and glazes. (page 26)

Sponge painting (above) is a simple faux finish. This technique can be tried on small projects such as the clock and candleholders and then on to larger surfaces such as walls. (page 26)

A brass plate and plaster bookend are aged with the help of Antiquing Wash and Chalk Paint. The candleholder is Antique-Washed with a warm golden shade.(page 26)

Three examples of faux finishes (rusted, verdigris and crackled) on identical garden pedestals.

Verdigris is reproduced by combining bronze and copper paint over turquoise. A brass bowl, metal recipe box and papier-mache box have all been finished to resemble the aged look of copper. (page 26)

Crackling simulates the look of aged and weathered paint. The frames and shaker basket depict two types of crackle finish. The tray is crackled and then decorated with a decoupaged botanical print. (page 27)

Wooden candleholders have been transformed into medieval artifacts using a rusting technique. Create the look of antiquity on any surface with this easy faux-finish. (page 27)

The wooden frame has been faux-rusted to give it a beautiful, aged, metallic appearance. (page 27)

Faux finishing techniques can be successfully accomplished by novice painters. This is especially true now because there are so many new and easy products available. There are even kits which make it easy to try the techniques on small projects before advancing to walls or other large surfaces.

Several small projects are included in this chapter for experimentation. Some examples of faux painted walls are in the previous chapter (Painting the Walls).

To be a faux artist you must first understand about paints and glazes.

Paints

Water based paints are recommended because they are odorless, quick-drying and clean up easily. They come in an endless variety of colors and shades.

Glazes

Water based glazes are also recommended. Glazes can be added to paint to slow down the drying time and to allow you to work and blend the paint.

With most faux finishes, you will first apply a coat of paint and then add a coat of glaze. While it's wet, this glaze is either ragged, sponged, flogged, dragged or bagged.

The directions for some of these finishes are in the following pages. If you try one or two of the faux finishes and are happy with the results, you might want to experiment further and become a real faux finish expert.

Wood Preparation

If your project is wood, follow the wood preparation instructions in Chapter 5.

SERPENTINE MARBLEIZING
Pictured on page 14.

Parson's Table (Ikea), Papier-mache Box (DC&C), Clay Pot, and Frame

Paint - Licorice, Summer Sky, Tartan Green, White
Extender
Thickener
Marbleizing sponge
Veining feather
Sponge brush
Sponge - kitchen type
Paper towels
Plastic foam plates
Spray bottle for water
Varnish - high gloss

Or use Marbleizing Kit (Plaid) Serpentine #30052INS

1. Apply basecoat (Licorice) using the sponge brush. Dry one hour. Sand (if necessary) and apply second coat. Dry for 24 hours.

2. Wet sponge, squeeze excess water. Tear edges of sponge with your fingernails.

3. Squeeze "Summer Sky" onto plate "palette" in thin strings as shown. Repeat with "Tartan Green", criss-crossing on top of the first color. Use four times more of the "Tartan Green" than the "Summer Sky".

4. Squeeze "Wicker White" onto the previous colors in the plate in the same way, but only go around the plate about 1/8 of a circle. Add 3 full circles of Thickener and 2 full circles of Extender on top of the other colors. Pick up plate and slightly tilt so that the colors gently roll together, but don't mix.

5. Gently place the torn side of the sponge in the mixture. Don't press down.

6. Lightly press sponge onto basecoated surface. Pick up and change position. Repeat, then reload every 3 - 5 presses. Some of the basecoated surface should keep showing. Continue to change direction of the sponge so you don't have a repeating pattern. Dry for 2 hours.

7. Apply about 1 teaspoon of "Wicker White" to new plate. On top of this apply about the same amount of Thickener and twice as much Extender. Roll together, but don't mix.

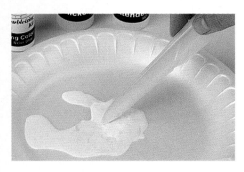

8. Drag wide part of feather tip through this mixture.

9. Start at upper left of project. Place tip of feather on surface and "drag-pull-twist-quiver" the feather diagonally across surface. Use a nervous and irregular movement mostly keeping the veins going in the same general direction (not criss-crossing or overlapping.)

10. Dry 24 hours and finish with high gloss protective sealer.

SPLASHED MARBLE

Pictured on page 14
Clay Pot, Clock (Walnut Hollow)

Splashing tool
Basecoat paint (Plaid) -
    Warm White
Clear Glaze
Colored Glaze (Plaid) - Soft Teal,
    Sage Green, New Gold Leaf
Alcohol
Spray bottle with water
Gold leaf paint
Small flat brush
Medium flat brush
1" sponge brush
Stippling brush

Or use Splashed Marble Kit (Plaid) #30080

1. Prepare the splashing tool. Remove the cap and tool tip. Use funnel to fill the tip with alcohol. Replace tip and cap.

2. Use the sponge brush to apply the Warm White. Let dry two hours, sand lightly and remove dust. Apply another coat of Warm White.

3. Brush a coat of Clear Glaze onto project. DO NOT LET DRY!

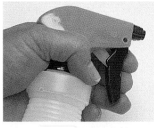

4. Spritz project with water from a spray bottle. The glaze should be moist, not runny.

5. While the surface is moist, use the tips of the Stippling Brush with Soft Teal glaze to "bounce and pound" randomly in the Clear glaze on the project. You should be able to see the basecoat color. Keep the brush vertical to the surface.

TIP

Use a damp cloth to wipe some of the glaze from the bristles of the brush before pouncing next color.

6. Apply Sage Green the same as the Soft Teal.

7. Apply New Gold Leaf. Apply less of this than the other colors. Apply over all colors, slightly overlapping the previous colors.

You want to see all three colors showing. Do not muddy the colors.

8. Spritz project with water from a spray bottle.

9. Splash alcohol over project. Turn the tool upside down and splash the project surface (shake the tool like a salt shaker). You will immediately see a reaction from the paints. They will start to water spot and separate, puddle and form craters. The project's appearance will vary by how much alcohol you splash. Wait 5 - 10 minutes and splash again with more alcohol.

10. When finished, detail the clock and the clay pot with the Gold Leaf paint using a small, flat brush (see photo on page 14). Seal the project with a matte varnish.

TIP

Use a blow dryer to speed up the drying time.

TORTOISESHELL

Pictured on page 15

Clock (Walnut Hollow), Papier-mache Box (DC&C), Jewelry Box with drawer, Frame

Paint - Antique Gold (Plaid) Gold Leaf Paint, Black

Glazes (Plaid) - Clear, Penny Copper, Black, New Gold Leaf

Sponge brush

Spray bottle for water

Bristle brush and Spouncer

Splashing tool

Alcohol

Varnish - satin

Or use Faux Finish Kit (Plaid) Tortoiseshell #30079

1. Prepare splashing tool by removing gold cap and tool tip. Use funnel to fill tool with alcohol. Replace tip and cap.

2. Use the sponge brush to apply a coat of Antique Gold. Let dry 2 hours. Sand lightly and remove dust. Apply another coat.

3. Brush a coat of Clear Glaze onto project. DO NOT LET DRY!

4. To create tortoiseshell, you will use a wet-on-wet process. It is very important to keep a spray bottle handy to mist the project with water if it starts to dry.

5. While the surface is moist, use the Spouncer to apply New Gold Leaf glaze to "spounce" or "bounce" randomly into the Clear glaze. You want to be able to still see the basecoat color. Rinse and blot the Spouncer.

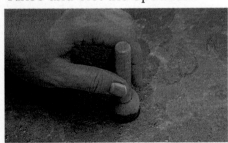

6. Apply Penny Copper over the moist Gold glaze. Rinse and blot the Spouncer.

7. Apply the Black the same way over the other two colors (you want to see all three colors showing. Do not muddy the colors).

8. Spritz with water from a spray bottle.

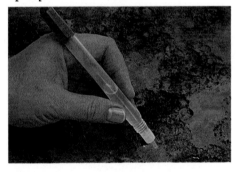

9. Turn the splashing tool upside-down and splash like a salt shaker. You will immediately see a reaction from the paints. They will start to water spot and separate, puddle, and form craters. The project's appearance will vary by how much alcohol you splash.

10. After splashing, you may still have some harsh circle edges left by the Spouncer. Use the bristle brush to eliminate these edges by mingling them together with the brush. Wait 5 - 10 minutes and splash again with more alcohol (you can add more glaze or alcohol splashes at any time to achieve your desired effect). Use a blow dryer to speed up the drying time AFTER the entire surface is finished. If your project surface is vertical, you will have to keep the paints a little dryer. This will lessen the water-splashed appearance.

11. Allow the surface to dry completely.

For clock and jewelry box:

12. Add Gold Leaf details to "bead feet" of clock and knob of jewelry box. (see page 15)

13. Paint a thin Black stripe on clock face and then paint the base Black.

14. Seal with a satin varnish.

PATINA

Pictured on page 15

Clock (Walnut Hollow), Papier-mache Box - DC&C, Jewelry Box with drawer, Frame

Paint - Red Oxide (Anita's)
Glazes - Metallic Gold, Dark
      Brown
Varnish - Semi-gloss
Sponge brush
Cotton rag
Bowl of water
Foam plastic plate
Plastic wrap
Old toothbrush
or use Patina kit (Backstreet)

1. Basecoat the surface with several applications of Red Oxide, letting dry between coats. Sand lightly between coats if necessary.

2. Shake Gold glaze vigorously for 60 seconds. Pour Gold glaze into a plate. Dip a glaze brush in water and stroke through the glaze in the plate to thin the consistency. Drag the brush across the Red Oxide basecoat. Stroke over the surface several times, building up layers of the thinned Gold glaze. Do not cover the Red Oxide basecoat entirely. Let dry. If the Gold seems too light in coverage, stroke on more Gold glaze and let dry 24 hours or longer.

3. Brush Dark Brown glaze over the surface. Using a cotton rag moistened with water, wipe away the Dark Brown glaze in any highlight areas. Allow the glaze to collect in any recessed or carved areas of the surface. You can also hit the wet glaze with a piece of wadded up plastic wrap for texture. Let dry 24 hours.

4. If desired, flyspeck the surface with a toothbrush loaded with Dark Brown glaze. Hold the toothbrush with the bristles pointing toward the project and run your finger across the bristles, causing specks of glaze to hit the project (be careful not to spatter your clothes or surrounding area). Let dry.

5. Apply one or more thin coats of the varnish to protect the finish.

MALACHITE

Pictured on page 16

Clock (Walnut Hollow), Box with drawers, Frame, Papier-mache box (DC&C)

Paint - (Plaid) Robin's Egg,
      Malachite Green
Gold Leaf paint
Glaze
Combing tool
Sponge brush
Piece of clean typing paper
Small brush for trim color
Varnish - matte finish
or use Combing Kit (Plaid)
#30076

1. Apply Robin's Egg. Let dry about 2 hours, sand lightly and remove dust. Apply another coat and let dry.

2. Apply glaze and then apply Malachite Green. DO NOT LET DRY!

3. Wad typing paper and press it into surface. This will eliminate the brush strokes.

4. Hold the comb firmly applying pressure to cut through the glaze.

5. There are several techniques that can be combed - straight, wavy, smooth combing or malachite stone combing.

Try to comb with one fluid motion, without lifting the comb.

Do not try to copy the look exactly. Each piece should have a look of its own.

Wipe the comb frequently with a paper towel.

6. Apply Gold Leaf paint to the knobs and edges of the jewelry box and seal with a matte finish.

COLOR WASHING

Pictured on page 17

Picket Fence Shelf

Acrylic paint - Cream, Light Charcoal

Master Quality Series Scumble Glazes - Serpentine Green, Aging Wash - Suncast

Brush - 1 1/2" all purpose paint brush

For knobs - Clear basecoat, iron basecoat, Instant Rust - (Modern Options)

Small brush

1. Remove drawers from shelf unit. Remove knobs from drawers and set aside.

2. Using light strokes in random places on shelf and drawer front, paint a few strokes of Charcoal paint following grain of wood. Allow to dry.

3. Using a mix of half water and half Cream paint, lightly "wash" shelf unit and drawer fronts with paint, allowing some wood grain and Charcoal strokes to show through. Allow to dry.

4. Following manufacturer's instructions, apply a light coat of Serpentine Green glaze and allow glaze to dry completely before proceeding. Glazes will take longer to dry than acrylic paints.

5. Complete shelf and drawer fronts by applying an overcoat of Suncast glaze. This glaze will mellow the colors and give an antique look to your piece. Allow to dry.

6. Drawer knobs: Following manufacturer's instructions, and using smaller paint brush, apply base coat, Iron paint and Instant Rust in this order, allowing each coat to dry before proceeding with the next.

7. Affix knobs to drawers.

SPONGING

Pictured on page 17

Clock (Walnut Hollow)
Wooden candleholders

Acrylic paint - Cream, Yellow, Medium Blue

Aging Wash (Master Quality Systems) Suncast

1 1/2" brush

Small section of sea sponge

Wooden candleholders

1. Apply an even basecoat of Cream paint to surface.

2. Using slightly moistened sponge, lightly dip in Yellow paint and dab color onto painted surface. Allow to dry.

3. Repeat step #2 to sponge Blue paint onto surface. Allow to dry.

4. Using paint brush, apply an even coat of Suncast glaze to surface. Allow glaze to dry.

Clock (Walnut Hollow)

1. Paint roof, base and perch of clock with a Blue basecoat.

2. Paint "walls" of clock Yellow and allow to dry.

3. Sponge Cream paint and alternative colors to roof, walls, perch and base of clock.

4. Apply Suncast glaze to all surfaces.

ANTIQUING WASH AND CHALKING

Plaster Bookend
Pictured on page 17

Antiquing Wash (Plaid) Hunter Green

Liquid Chalk (Plaid) Patina

Bisque Candleholder (Westcoast Ceramics)
Pictured on page 17.

Antiquing Wash (Plaid) Metallic Honey Gold

Hammered Brass Wall Plaque
Pictured on page 17

Liquid Chalk (Plaid) Patina

1. Spray Antiquing Wash on the project. Wipe off excess with soft, damp cloth. Let dry. Then brush on Liquid Chalk and wipe off the raised areas allowing it to remain in crevices.

VERDIGRIS

Pictured on page 19

Metal Recipe Box, Papier mache Box (DC&C), Brass Bowl

Paint (Backstreet) Copper

Glazes (Backstreet) Light Verdigris, Verdigris

Bristle brush

Sea sponge

Sponge brush

Old toothbrush

Paper plates

Varnish - matte finish

or use Verdigris kit (Backstreet)

1. Paint the project with the Copper basecoat. Let dry and apply another coat. Apply a third coat if needed.

2. Shake the glaze about 60 seconds. Dampen a sea sponge and squeeze out excess water. Dab the sponge into Verdigris glaze then dab the sponge in an empty plate several times to distribute the glaze evenly.

3. Dab the project randomly with the sponge. Dip the sponge in water and dab over the wet glaze. Allow some of the Verdigris to run down the surface.

4. Pour Light Verdigris into a paper plate. Load the sea sponge with Light Verdigris glaze. Sponge on the project surface as a highlight color. Do not cover as much areas as when applying the first Verdigris glaze. Again, dip the sponge in water and dab over the wet glaze. Let dry at least 24 hours or longer depending on the climate conditions in your area.

5. Build up a second layer of color by repeating the applications of Verdigris and Light Verdigris. Remember to keep hints of the Copper basecoat showing through the layers of glaze.

6. To complete the Verdigris look, load an old toothbrush with Light Verdigris glaze. Hold with the bristles pointing toward

the project and run your finger across the bristles causing specks of glaze to hit the project. Let dry 24 hours.

7. Apply one or two coats of varnish to protect the finish.

Crackling
Pictured on page 19
Frames
Shaker Basket

Crackling medium (Delta) for frames & basket
Two contrasting combinations of paint: Gold and Red, (frames and basket), Wisteria and Hunter Green (frame)
Paint brush
Sponge brush
Varnish

1. Apply basecoat (Red or Hunter Green) to project and let dry.

2. Apply one light, even coat of crackle with firm brush strokes. Let it become tacky, but not dry.

3. Brush on one light, even coat of the second color (Gold or Wisteria) Topcoat will begin to crack within minutes. Cracks will follow the direction of topcoat brush strokes. Apply topcoat in criss-cross pattern for a more random effect.

4. When dry, seal with varnish.

Wooden Tray (Wooden Hen)
Pictured on page 19
Paint (Decoart) Hauser Dark

Green, Light Buttermilk
Crackling medium
8 1/2" x 11" floral print for decoupage
Decoupage medium
Varnish - matte finish
Sponge brush

Or: Crackling Kit (Decoart)

1. Use the same directions as frames and basket using the Light Buttermilk for basecoat and Hauser Dark Green for topcoat.

2. After topcoat has dried completely, start the decoupage process.

3. With a sponge brush, apply decoupage medium to the center of tray. Then apply medium to the back of the paper you will be using. Apply the paper to the tray. Smooth down and then sponge on decoupage medium over the top of the image. With fingers, smooth any wrinkles or extra medium from the paper. (Prick with pin if any air bubbles.)

4. Let dry. Apply 2 or 3 more coats of decoupage medium, allowing to dry between each coat.

5. Seal with a matte varnish.

Rusting
Pictured on page 20
Wooden Frame, Wooden Candleholders, Wooden Pedestals
Basecoat - Instant Iron

Top coat - Liquid Rust (Modern Options)

Paint brush

1. Follow manufacturer's instructions for applying.

S·T·E·N·C

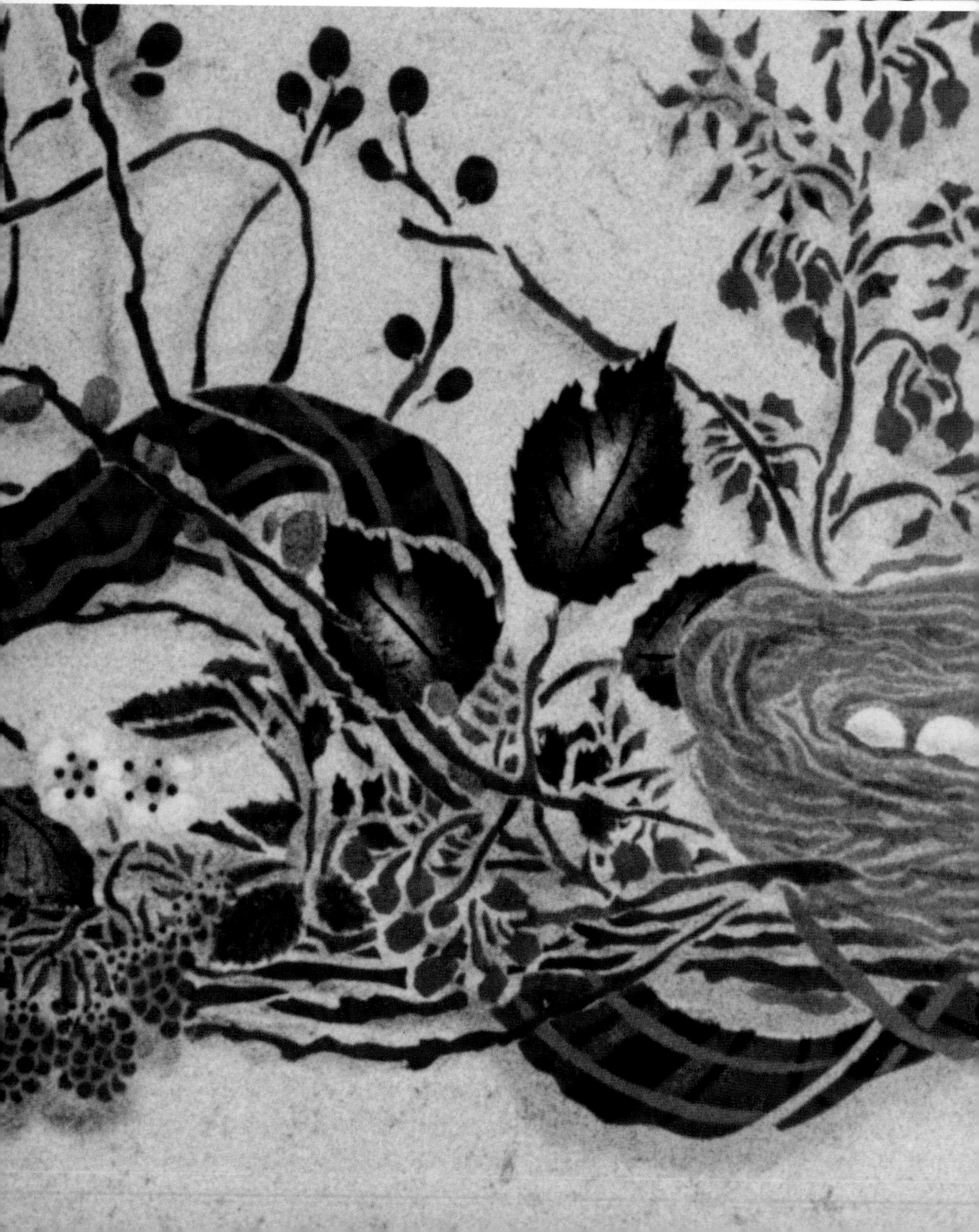

·I·L·I·N·G

The art of stenciling has been used
for hundreds of years to decorate
everything from walls to pottery.

Commonplace items become
memorable decor with the addition of
stenciled designs. Victorian motifs
add sweet charm to a hat box, blue
and white china decorate a "tea
cabinet" and a garden bench is
transformed with the addition of
roses and flowing ribbons.

A few supplies and a little inspiration
are all you need to get started!

Stencil a soft green heart-shaped topiary on this mini-cupboard. Use it to keep household keys handy and out of sight.
(page 36)

Dappled sunlight adds charming nostalgia to a garden bench stenciled with soft pink roses and fluttering blue ribbons. Use the rose-bordered frame to surround a cherished photo.
(page 36)

Victorian hats are stenciled on a papier-mache box, then embellished with ribbons and antique paper lace. The perfect place for storing a precious hat or other treasures.
(page 36)

Stenciled garden designs add charm to a rustic watering can and an aged metal container - unique planters for trailing ivy, bright annuals or often-used garden tools. Delicate ivy decorates the papier mache book/box - a place to store seeds or special gardening notes.
(page 36)

Capture the memories of treasured vacations and
childhood camping trips. Choose northwest
motifs from this selection of rustic designs and
stencil your very own hideaway.

(page 37)

Create a setting for an antique buffet with
a stenciled wall motif of wispy twigs,
bird's nest and ribbons. Warmly glowing
lamplight enhances the stenciled leaves
on the background wall.

(page 37)

Lacy, deep green ferns and
colorful bird-of-paradise are
just two of the exotic designs
used to convert this corner
into a cozy, magical retreat.

(page 36)

Stenciled blue and white china images on a white chest evoke memories of tea parties and gentler times. This "tea chest" stores tea bags, table linens, sugar cubes and silverware - essentials for setting an elegant table for a cozy afternoon tea.
(page 36)

The wonderful thing about stenciling is that with the slightest bit of practice anyone can create beautiful designs.

Start with a small project and then graduate to a more complicated design, improving your skills as you go. When you've completed two or three small projects, you can then move on to stenciling walls.

Supplies:

Stencils - available in every size, shape and design imaginable

Paints - Acrylics, Dry Brush Paints, or Stencil Crayons

Brushes - Stencil brushes are wood handled with round, stiff bristles. They come in various sizes. Be sure to use this type of brush for stenciling projects.

Stencil rollers - small paint rollers used to cover large background areas

Sponge brushes or sponges - can be used to create a sponged effect.

Spray adhesive or painter's tape for applying stencils to project. (Painter's tape is preferred.)

Miscellaneous supplies:

Brush cleaner
Palette (or paper plate)
Paper towels
Tack cloth
Q-Tips (for correcting mistakes)
Practice paper (shelf liner works well - for practicing techniques or trying out color combinations).

Terms you need to know:

Overlay - Some stencils come with only one part, but others that are more intricate, come in groups - one sheet for each color. They are used in a certain order to create the designs.

Mirror Image - a design that has been stenciled on the reverse side to create facing images.

Registration Marks - dotted lines or holes on overlay stencils that are used for alignment.

Getting started:

1. Tape the stencil to the object to be painted. Apply paint to brush and then dab the brush on a paper towel so that the brush is almost dry.

2. Hold brush vertically and use either a dabbing or swirling motion. Start at the edges of the stencil while you have more paint on your brush and let it get lighter (less paint) towards the center. This will give you a shaded effect.

3. For another effect, use a sponge for painting and use a dabbing action. This will give a mottled, textured effect, great for trees and foliage.

4. When using overlays, allow paint to dry between each application.

5. When finished painting, peel away the stencil before the paint is completely dry - this will prevent the paint from cracking.

Topiary Mini Cupboard

Pictured on page 30

Mini cupboard
Stencil (Back Street) "Topiary Garden" #17934
Paint - Pale Green, Medium Green, Dark Green, Pink, Light Terra Cotta, Medium Terra Cotta
Brushes: Stencil brush, small liner brush, 1/2" Flat brush, sponge brush

1. With sponge brush, basecoat cupboard using Light Green.

2. Stencil following photo for color placement.

3. Paint Dark Green checks on edge of cupboard with a 1/2" flat brush.

4. To make the tiny flowers at the top, use the wooden end of the liner brush to make little Pink dots. Then use a liner brush to make Green leaves.

5. Lightly antique the edges of the cupboard using the Dark Green paint. Sponge on a little of the paint and immediately wipe off with a soft cloth.

6. Apply matte varnish if desired.

White Garden Bench

Pictured on page 30

Garden Bench (A Place in the Garden)

Stencil (American Traditional) Rose

Paint (Plaid) Dry Brush Stencil Paint - Bouquet Pink, Dusty Rose, Fern Green, Forest Shade, Quilt Blue

Stencil brushes

1. Stencil the rose design on the back of the bench as pictured. To create shading, use Dusty Rose and dab repeatedly in the shaded areas. Do the same with Fern Green and Forest Green.

Rose Frame

Pictured on page 30

Frame

Stencil (Plaid) Designer Tape - "Roses"

Paint - Off-White acrylic basecoat

Stencil Paint (Plaid) - Bouquet Pink, Dusty Rose, Fern Green, Truffles Brown

Stencil Brush

Sponge Brush

Sand paper

Varnish - matte

1. Basecoat frame using the Off-White acrylic paint. Let dry.

2. To distress the frame, sand edges until it has an aged look.

3. Designer Tape has adhesive on the back and comes in a continuous roll. Cut off a section of rose with leaves and branch. Apply the stencil tape on the parts of the frame where design is desired. Paint using a stencil brush. Move the stencil to the next position and re-apply.

4. When dry, seal with a matte varnish.

Rusted Watering Can

Pictured on page 30

Watering Can (Kraft Klub)

Stencil (Back Street) Bird's Nest Section of "Let Your Garden Grow"

Paint - (Plaid) Fern Green, Forest Shade, Ecru Lace, Blue Chintz

Stencil Brush

1. Tape the stencil to watering can and paint using the colors listed above. Allow to dry between each application.

Rusted Planter

Pictured on page 30

Planter (Kraft Klub)

Stencil (Plaid) Folk Art Painter's Stencil - "Garden Angel"

Stencil (Delta) Ivy border

Paint - Green, Gold

Stencil brush

1. Tape ivy stencil to bottom edge of planter and paint Green. Let dry.

2. Tape trellis section of "Garden Angel" stencil to front of planter and paint Gold.

Book / Box

Pictured on page 30

Papier-Mache Book/Box (Kraft Klub)

Stencil (Delta) Ivy Border

Paint - Green

Stencil Brush

1. Using a small stencil brush, stencil the ivy design along the left edge of the box.

Blue China Tea Chest

Pictured on page 34

Stencil (Plaid) "Tea Time" #26674

Stencil (Plaid) "Gingham Border" #26724

Chest of drawers (Ikea)

Paint - White acrylic

Dry Brush Stencil Paint (Plaid) - Ship's Fleet Navy, Blue Chintz

1. Basecoat chest White (two to three coats.)

2. Stencil drawers with plates and tea pots, reversing some of the stencils (as pictured). Be sure to wipe off stencils before using the reverse side.

3. Stencil the sides of the chest using the gingham stencil. Follow the directions for the gingham on the package.

Victorian Hat Box

Pictured on page 31

Stencil (Plaid) "Victorian Hats" #26708

Paint - White acrylic

Dry Brush Stencil Paints (Plaid) Ecru Lace, Dusty Rose, Vintage, Burgundy, Forest Shade, Fern Green

Stencil brushes

Sponge brush

Papier-Mache Box (DC&C) 40" round, 8" deep

Ribbon - 1 1/2 yards Burgundy Moire, 7/8" wide

1 1/2 yards Hunter Green Velvet, 7/8" wide

Paper Lace Trim (MPR) Ivory

1. Basecoat the box using a sponge brush and the White acrylic.

2. Follow the directions in the package to stencil. (Cut off the lace part of the stencil.)

3. Glue the paper lace to the top edge of box and the burgundy ribbon over the top of the paper lace.

4. Glue the Hunter Green ribbon to the bottom edge of the box.

Rustic Cabin
Pictured on page 32

Stencils (Jan Dressler) Rainier Lodge Collection
Paints - Listed on the individual stencils
Stencil Brushes

1. Choose the motifs from the collection.

2. Follow the instructions on the individual stencils.

Briar Patch Wall
Pictured on page 33

Stencils (Jan Dressler) Hickory Hollow Briar Patch #402 and Bumbleberry Wallpaper Repeat #428
Paint - listed on the individual stencils
Stencil brushes

1. Follow the instructions on the individual stencils you select to create your own Briar Patch wall.

Garden Bedroom
Pictured on page 33

Stencils (Jan Dressler) Moroccan Tassels #167, Greek Column #160, Bird of Paradise #608, Stone Block Wall #633, Palm #651
Paint - listed on the individual stencil packages.
Stencil brushes

Stenciling Tips
from Jan Dressler
of Jan Dressler Designs

Practice your technique on paper first. This will acquaint you with the application technique, and help you to establish your combination of colors.

Finish a practice print and tape it to the wall, then step back to see that the colors you've chosen will work.

When stenciling, use a large brush for large openings. This will avoid a polka dot effect and also make the job go faster. Use smaller brushes for delicate work.

To clean stencil after use - lay it on a layer of newspaper and spray with Formula 409 to wet the stencil. Then put it in a poly bag and let it soak. It can be easily washed off later. Or use rubbing alcohol and a sponge to swirl off the paint.

Clean brushes before paint has completely dried. Use Murphy's Oil Soap or dish detergent. If paint has dried on the brush, pour Formula 409 or regular isopropyl alcohol in zip-lock bag with the brushes bristle-side down. When you wash them, the paint just washes away. Let brushes dry thoroughly before you use them again.

Make a portable work table on your ladder to keep from climbing up and down. Fold in flaps of a cardboard box and fit it over the top step of ladder. Tape down paper plate with paint on it and paper towel. Wear a carpenter's belt for your brushes.

Use fabric paints for stenciling on fabrics. Prewash fabric. Cottons work best for permanence of paint.

Stenciling Corners: Run 1/2" painter's tape down each wall, right at corner. Then stencil right over the tape. When it's removed, a nice clean break is made.

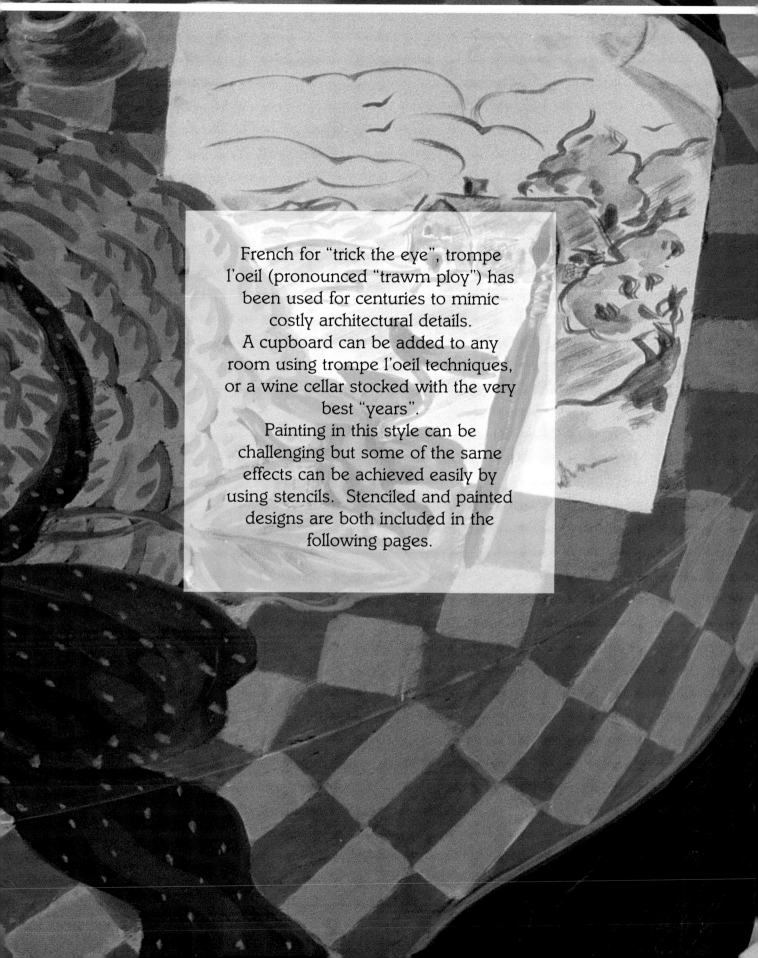

French for "trick the eye", trompe l'oeil (pronounced "trawm ploy") has been used for centuries to mimic costly architectural details.

A cupboard can be added to any room using trompe l'oeil techniques, or a wine cellar stocked with the very best "years".

Painting in this style can be challenging but some of the same effects can be achieved easily by using stencils. Stenciled and painted designs are both included in the following pages.

No longer a blank wall, this cleverly captured wooden cupboard with its open door has a handy "slip of paper" taped to its facade for reminders. The "note" is treated with chalk paint to permit adding and changing real messages. The hatbox is also woodgrained and features the same hinges and lock as the cupboard.
(page 44)

Has the artist left her hat and unfinished sketch
behind? This whimsical example of trompe l'oeil
truly "fools the eye". For a great conversation
starter, add this wonderful hat box to a den or
gathering place for family and friends.
(page 45)

Sewing essentials that are never stored away grace the top of this cabinet. Even spectacles for close work are handy! Some of the buttons are real, some are painted. Can you tell the difference?

(page 45)

Tip- Faux Finish techniques make perfect backgrounds for Tromp L'oeil stenciled designs.

This elegant wine cellar just looks like it contains a collection of vintage bottles. Is this wishful thinking or a perfectly wonderful focal point at the end of a hallway? Start by stenciling a few bottles and then add more just as if you were amassing a real wine collection. (page 45)

The bathroom below has been decorated with a combination of "real life" creatures and prehistoric petroglyphs. A fossilized shell adds interest to this medley of trompe l'oeil stencils.(page 45)

The paintings in this chapter are so life-like that the viewer may attempt to reach for an object before realizing that it's just a painted image.

Much study and practice is required for this style of painting. As an alternative, stenciling can give the same effect with little or no training. The stencils used usually have multiple overlays that help create realism. Depth and perspective are added by using shading and highlighting techniques. After stenciling, the shadows are added.

Both techniques are illustrated in this chapter. For instance, the painter's hatbox and the realistic cupboard are hand-painted. The wine cellar and sewing cabinet are stenciled.

For the hand painted technique you will need:

Full sized drawing of the objects, including the shadows
Drawing paper
Pencil
Ruler
Graphite paper
Acrylic paints
Brushes - flat shader and liner
For stenciling, you will need:
Pre-cut stencils with multiple
    overlays
Painter's tape
Acrylic paints or Dry Brush
    Stencil paints
Stencil brushes
(see Stencil Chapter for more details)

Some information about:
Scale - Objects should be painted the size they would normally appear to the viewer. Objects look smaller the farther

away they are. If an image is to be viewed at close range, it should be painted life-size.

Perspective - Perspective is very important in achieving the realism of trompe l'oeil. There are many books on this subject for reference.

Shading - Determine an imaginary light source and add highlights and shadows to the painted image in reference to that light. For simple trompe l'oeil effects, paint each object in one color tone. Then add highlights by mixing White paint into that color. Paint shadows by mixing Black paint into the original color.

Cupboard

Pictured on page 40
Paint (Plaid) Camel, Apple Butter, Brown, Black, Gray, Yellow Ochre, White
Glaze Medium
Grainer Tool
Sponge brush
Small round brush

1. Measure the area on the wall to be painted and then make a pattern by using this measurement and enlarging and photocopying the cupboard in the photo on Page 40.

2. Trace this pattern to the wall.

3. Follow the instructions for the "wood grained hat box" for wood graining.

4. To paint the lock, hinges and note, use patterns on Page 46. Trace these onto the cupboard.

5. Paint the lock and hinges using Black with Gray shadows.

6. For note: Basecoat with White Chalk Paint (if desired) or

regular acrylic. Paint shadows with a mixture of White with a little Yellow Ochre and Black.

Wood Grained Hat Box
Pictured on page 40
Papier-Mache Box (DC&C)
Paint (Plaid) Camel, Apple Butter Brown, Charcoal Black, Gray
Glaze Medium
Grainer Tool

1. Basecoat with the Camel paint. Spray lightly with water. Wait a few minutes and pull color slowly with a dry foam brush. Don't over brush.

2. Let dry completely and then mix Apple Butter Brown with the glaze medium. Brush on glaze in various directions, dabbing brush in some areas as you go.

3. Take grainer and pull through the glaze, rocking back and forth. Add in fine grain where desired.

4. Use dry brush to soften grain lines. To create depth - don't soften all grains.

5. When dry, do a final antique wash with acrylics or use a wood stain and let dry.

6. When dry, trace on pattern for hinges. Paint the hinges using Black and Gray for shadows. Mix White with Gray for highlights.

Painter's Hat Box
Pictured on page 41
Wooden box (13 1/2" x 18")
Paint (acrylics) Navy Blue, Forest Green, Light Tan, Medium Tan, Light Brown, Cream, Burnt Sienna, Medium Red, Medium Yellow, Medium Green, Light Green, Medium Blue, Cobalt Blue, Light Gray, Medium Orange, Bright Yellow

Crackling Medium (Delta)
Brushes - 1" sponge brush
    1/4" flat
    1 medium round
Graphite paper
Pencil

. Enlarge pattern 200% or to fit
our project.

. Transfer design to box
pattern on page 46). Continue
ablecloth design around edge of
ox.

. Using the sponge brush,
asecoat the bottom area of box
under tablecloth) Forest Green.

. Apply Crackle medium to this
rea according to manufacturer's
nstructions.

. Apply a topcoat of Navy Blue
o crackle area.

. Using round brush, work in a
ircular motion beginning at
enter of hat, loosely brushing
ight Tan strokes to simulate
voven straw.

. Add Medium Tan for
hadows on the lighter strokes.

. Use Brown to give spaces in-
etween "straw" strokes some
hadow and definition, filling in
aps as you go.

. Paint bow Navy Blue and add
trokes of Gray mixed with a
ouch of Navy to simulate
hadows and give ribbon
oftness. Dot ribbon with Cream
aint (use end of brush dipped
n paint).

0. Paint checkerboard pattern
n tablecloth using Bright Yellow
nd Cobalt Blue. Use brush
eely and allow irregularities.

1. Outline the tablecloth's outer
dge with one border of Gray
ixed with a touch of Green and

another border of Light Blue.

12. Paint bottles Green using
round brush. Paint highlights
with Green mixed with White
and shade with Green mixed
with Blue.

13. Paint flower Orange, leaves
and stem near hat, Green.

14. Using Cream, paint "sketch
paper" and Gray for shadow
areas. Using tip of round brush -
paint or sketch "landscape with
cottage" on the sketch paper.
(See photo for suggested colors.)

15. Finish with matte varnish.

Sewing Cabinet
Pictured on page 42
Wooden cabinet with drawers
    (Ikea)
Stencil (Jan Dressler)
    "Conscious Clutter"
Paints - colors listed on stencil
    package
Paint for cabinet (Plaid Durable
    Colors) Mojave Sunset
Glaze (Plaid) Bark Brown
Plastic bags
Brushes - Sponge brush, stencil
    brushes

1. Sand cabinet. Wipe away
dust.

2. Basecoat drawers and chest
with Mojave Sunset.

3. When dry, brush on the Bark
Brown glaze to one drawer at a
time - work quickly as paint dries
fast. Use a plastic bag balled up
to spounce on the glaze, getting
a nice even texture. Then glaze
each side of the chest and
spounce with the plastic bag.
Try to use areas of the bag
where no glaze has collected (or
have 2 or 3 bags handy).

4. Stencil the clutter on the

cabinet using the images desired.
On the cabinet (page 42) the
spectacles, scissors, skein of
floss and buttons have been
used. Follow the photograph on
the stencil package to copy
highlights and shadowing.

5. When paint is dry, finish with
a matte varnish.

Wine Cellar
Pictured on page 43
Stencil (Jan Dressler) Wine Rack
    #396
Stencil paints (colors are listed
on the stencil package)
Stencil brushes

(Note: This design contains 8
overlays. The cabinet is done by
reversing the stencil of the same
rack.

1. Find a nice, blank wall. This
design is 81" high and 33" wide.

2. Follow the instructions on the
stencil package to paint this wine
cellar on your wall. The bottles
are separate and can be
stenciled randomly to stock your
wine rack.

Trompe l'oeil Petroglyphs
Pictured on page 43
Stencils (Jan Dressler) Lizard
    #554, Sea Fossils #387,
    Lascaux Cave paintings #380
Paint (colors listed on the stencil
packages)
Stencil brushes

1. Add these petroglyph stencils
to decorate walls within your
own home. Choose any
combination of the stencils to
create your own private
archeological retreat.

Enlarge 200%

P·A·I·N·T·I·N·G

Every culture from Chinese to Scandinavian, European to Early American, developed a distinctive style of painted furniture. This rich blend of cultures has evolved into a mix of colors, designs, and textures, more suited to our present-day lifestyle.

Whether spray painting wicker furniture, decorating a child's room or stenciling a kitchen table, painting can give new life to family heirlooms, garage sale finds, or flea market bargains.

Brighten any room of the house by trying some of these easy techniques.

What a difference paint makes! The same desk and chair have been painted three different ways to show the various styles and moods that can be created with just a change of color combinations.   These effects can easily be achieved to fit any decorating scheme. (page 59)

A kitchen nook with its painted table and chairs takes on the colors of the wonderful collection of pottery.

A narrow, stenciled table fits snugly under a coordinated plate rack. A perfect place for a quick meal for two.

Create a romantic retreat so delightful that you never want to leave. The Victorian wicker bed is painted a delightful Leafy Green to coordinate with the pretty linens.
(page 60)

To evoke nostalgia for a kinder and gentler time, decorate with Victorian wicker. This lacy chair has been painted a Light Sage. The basket, holding a leafy plant, is Grape to match the chair cushion.
(page 60)

Refinishing Wicker

Wicker needs to be repainted occasionally:

1. Remove any flakes with a wire brush.

2. If this isn't successful (or if the piece is an antique), have the furniture professionally stripped. Do not use commercial paint stripper because it tends to break down the wicker.

3. Spray several thin coats of latex enamel paint, letting dry between each coat.

Don't throw that rusty old wagon away! Repaint it in these fun colors and add it to a child's room filled with toys and games.
(page 61)

The teddy bears love their special tea party furniture. Muted hues of rose and green are adapted from the tea set. Stylized tea cup and silverware designs are stamped on the table top and matching chairs. It will always be tea time in this special place.
(page 60)

Bright colors enliven children's furnishings. Tempered with black and white, the use of patterns, dots, stars and vintage Dick and Jane illustrations, create a story-book setting. Chalkboard paint turns a simple stool into a game board or message center.
(page 60)

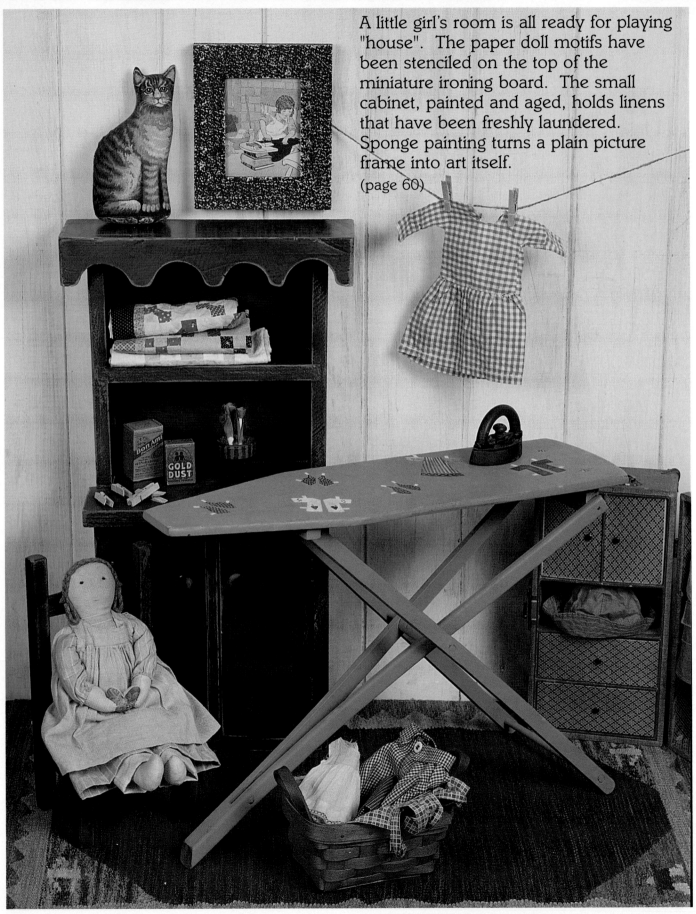

A little girl's room is all ready for playing "house". The paper doll motifs have been stenciled on the top of the miniature ironing board. The small cabinet, painted and aged, holds linens that have been freshly laundered. Sponge painting turns a plain picture frame into art itself.

(page 60)

Refinishing Outdoor Metal Furniture

Any metal furniture left outdoors for long periods of time will rust. To rescue one of these relics from your garage (or a garage sale):

1. Clean with steel wool or a fine wire brush

2. Use a rust remover.

3. For tough jobs, use a rust stripper.

4. For really tough jobs, have the piece professionally sandblasted.

5. Paint with a good rust-resistant outdoor paint. These are available in sprays and cans.

Enjoy alfresco dining in the cool shade of your own patio. This handsome cast iron patio set has been rejuvenated with the help of a little rust remover and a brand new coat of Hunter Green paint.

(page 61)

Combine soft blue, touches of pastel pink and white for a contemporary finish to country-style furniture. Accessorize the room to match the paint choices, or let the paint take the lead. Accent colors on the chair and small stand add interest.

(page 60)

Painting Chairs

1. Turn chair upside-down. Paint legs, then seat bottom.

2. When legs are dry, turn chair right side up and paint the back.

3. Then paint seat.

Freshen up home decor by repainting old furniture, or buy an unfinished piece and paint to suit the room. Select the effect you'd like and the colors you prefer, then visit your paint store. A wide variety of paint colors and types are available.

Don't be afraid to be bold when selecting your colors. Color combinations can set your style, and evoke a certain mood.

You can achieve a decorator look with just a few strokes of your brush.

General Instructions for painting unfinished furniture

1. Sand the piece so that it is smooth and free of any rough spots.

2. Remove sand dust with a tack cloth.

3. Use a wood sealer on porous surfaces. You'll want to use an acrylic paint so that clean-up will be easy.

4. Paint using a sponge brush or a bristle brush. The better the brush you use, the smoother the paint job will be.

5. Paint one or two coats and then decide if the piece needs a third coat. This will depend on the quality of paint and how porous the wood is.

6. If using more than one color of paint, mask off certain areas so that the job will be neat and crisp. Use painter's tape for best results.

7. Be sure to varnish your piece after the paint dries. You may choose a matte, semi-gloss or high-gloss varnish depending on

the result you want. The varnish will seal the paint and protect your piece of furniture.

Refinishing painted furniture

If you've purchased an old piece of furniture at a swap meet or garage sale that looks as if it has 30 coats of paint, you'll have to strip (or remove) all of the paint in order to paint on a fresh coat and have the piece look new.

Stripping is a tedious job, but well worth the effort (especially if you've gotten a real bargain on the piece of furniture).

Note - never, ever, ever remove the paint from a real antique piece. The piece is much more valuable with its original paint. When you are in doubt as to whether or not it's an antique, have it appraised by a reputable antique dealer.

1. Using an old bristle brush, apply paint remover to small areas of the piece. When the paint starts to bubble, use a scraper to scrape it off. A plastic or wooden scraper works best. (be careful not to harm the wood, unless you want an aged and distressed look). Then go to another area of the piece and repeat this process. (Be sure to follow all of the directions on the label.) You will want to do this job in a very well-ventilated area because of the fumes. Also, be sure to wear rubber gloves to protect your hands.

2. After most of the paint is removed, you can then sand the piece until it's smooth, removing any stubborn paint that may remain.

3. Dispose of any rags used for stripping, to avoid fire hazard.

4. Then follow instructions above for painting your piece.

Three Desks
Pictured on page 50

1. Follow the general instructions above for preparing and painting the desk and chair. (All have been painted with American Accents Paints)
The three color combinations pictured are listed as follows:

a. Nature's hues
Leafy Green, Summer Squash

b. Traditional
Colonial Red, Teal, Taupe

c. Colonial
Claret Wine, Midnight Blue, Nutmeg

Table, Chairs and Plate Rack
Pictured on page 51

Acrylic paint (American Accents)
        Leafy Green, Light Sage, Grape
Stencil - Swirl design
Paint brush and stencil brush
Painter's tape

1. Prepare wood to be painted following general instructions.

2. Paint table (refer to photo).

3. After paint dries, you are ready to stencil. Hold stencil firmly against the surface of table or attach with painter's tape.

4. Dip stencil brush into paint and wipe off excess on a paper towel.

5. Apply the brush to the stencil using a dabbing motion until area is filled.

F·U·R·N·I·T·U·R·E

6. Repeat stenciling across the table as pictured. You may wish to stencil the top of the table in a coordinating color.

7. Paint plate rack Leafy Green to match table.

8. Chairs are painted Light Sage with Grape.

Windsor Chair and Shelf
Pictured on page 58

Chair and shelf
Paint (American Accents) -
Antique Blue, White Wash,
    Cottage Rose
Paint brushes

1. Paint the chair Antique Blue.

2. Accent details of chair in Cottage Rose (as pictured).

3. Paint the shelf White Wash and the top Antique Blue.

4. Paint the drawer Cottage Rose

Wicker Bed and Table
Pictured on page 52

Paint (American Accents) Leafy
    Green

1. Follow instructions for painting wicker furniture (page 53).

Wicker Chair
Pictured on page 53
Paint (American Accents) Light
    Sage

1. Follow instructions for painting wicker furniture (page 53)

Tea Time Table and Chairs
Pictured on page 54

Table and Chairs (Ikea)
Paint (Plaid Durable Colors) -
    Rose, Green Mist
Foam Stamps (Back Street
    Chunky Stamps)
    Tea cups, silverware
Sponge brush
(This set comes unassembled.
Paint before assembling)

1. Sand lightly and remove dust.

2. Paint following the photo (or use your own combinations). You will need two to three coats.

3. Apply paint to the stamps using a sponge brush and stamp randomly on the table top and also on the chairs, if desired.

4. Use a matte varnish to seal.

5. Assemble the furniture following manufacturer's instructions.

Doll's Ironing Board
Pictured on page 56

Ironing Board (found at an antique store - but new ones are available at Ikea)
Stencils (Plaid Folk Art Painter's
    Stencils) #1070
Paint (Plaid Dry Brush Stencil
    Paints) - White Linen,
    Sherwood Forest Green,
    Ol'' Pioneer Red, Ship's
    Fleet Navy, Wildflower
    Honey
Sponge brush
Stencil brush
Small liner brush for details

1. Paint ironing board the color of your choice.

2. When dry, start stenciling.

3. Use the stencils to trace a pattern on a test piece of paper prior to stenciling to get the placement right.

4. Using a small stencil brush, paint the large elements first. Let dry and then add the smaller details.

5. Sand edges of ironing board for an aged look, if desired.

Frame, Mini Cabinet, Chair
Pictured on page 56

Wooden frame
Doll cabinet
Doll Chair
Paint - (acrylic) Forest Green,
    Ecru
Sponge brush
Sand paper

1. Paint the frame Green and then sponge using Ecru paint. Add illustration of your choice.

2. Paint the doll cabinet and chair Forest Green.

3. When dry, sand the edges to give an aged look.

Blackboard Step Stool
Pictured on page 55

Wooden Step Stool (Wooden
    Hen)
Acrylic paint - White, Black, Red,
    Gold, Turquoise
Blackboard Paint (Backstreet) -
    Black
Star stencil (Aleene's)
Sponge brush
Stencil brush
3/4" flat brush for stripes

1. Sand stool.

2. Paint following the photo (or use your own color scheme).

3. Paint the sides of the stool using the blackboard paint. Follow the manufacturer's instructions for curing the "blackboard" so it will be ready for the chalk.

4. Stencil stars on the top of the stool.

P·A·I·N·T·I·N·G

A Child's Frame
Pictured on page 55

Frame
Acrylic paint - Red, Cream
Sea sponge
Sponge brush
Paper plate

1. Using sponge brush, paint the frame two coats of Red. Let dry.

2. Dip sea sponge in the Cream paint (use a paper plate) and sponge lightly over the whole frame.

3. Add a print or photo of your choice.

Alphabet Stool
Pictured on page 55

Wooden stool
Acrylic paint - Gold, Blue, Turquoise, Green, White, Black
Stamps - alphabet stamps
Sponge brush
1/2" wide flat brush

1. Turn the stool upside down and paint the legs first. You'll probably need two coats. Paint each section a different color (see photo). Mask off each section with tape.

2. Add the dots by dipping the wooden end of the brush in the white paint and touching it to the wood.

3. Paint the Black and White stripes with the 1/2" wide brush.

4. When the legs are dry, turn right side up and paint the seat.

5. When paint is dry, randomly stamp with alphabet stamps.

6. Varnish to seal.

Dick and Jane Storage Chest
Pictured on page 55

Storage Chest (Ikea)
Acrylic paint - Red, Black
Wood sealer
Color copy from children's book
Decoupage medium
Alphabet stamps
Sponge brush
Varnish

1. Sand storage chest and remove dust.

2. Apply wood sealer, if desired.

3. Paint the chest Red (or color of your choice).

4. Make a pattern using one of the drawers. Cut color copies using the pattern.

5. Apply decoupage medium to the back of the picture for the first drawer. Carefully place it in position on the drawer. Apply a coat of decoupage medium on top of this. While it's still wet, smooth it with your fingers, pushing out any air bubbles. Add as many coats as desired.

6. Do the same to all the drawers. You may need to trim the pictures after they've dried with a craft knife.

7. Apply varnish to seal. Use the box to store pencils, crayons, markers and other treasures.

Cast Iron Patio Furniture
Pictured on page 57

Rust remover (Rust-Oleum) - Rust Reformer
Paint (Rust-Oleum) - "Stops Rust" spray paint - Hunter Green
Metal brush

1. Remove rust using a metal brush and/or Rust Reformer which converts the rust to a smooth, paintable surface; no need to sand. Apply following manufacturer's instructions.

2. If the piece is very rusty, you might try Rust Stripper (by Rust-Oleum) which removes the heaviest rust and leaves a clean metal surface.

3. Protect surroundings.

4. Paint with green spray paint.

Checkered Wagon
Pictured on page 55

Rust remover (Rust Oleum) Rust Reformer
Spray paint (Rust-Oleum) "Stops Rust" Sunburst Yellow and Gloss Black
Paint (Rust-Oleum) can of "Stops Rust" Gloss Black
Masking tape
Paint brush

1. Remove rust using Rust Reformer.

2. Prepare wagon and surrounding area for spray painting. Wrap and tape slitted trash bags around wheels and handle.

3. Spray wagon Sunburst Yellow (2 coats).

4. Mask off squares around edge of wagon using masking tape. Spray Black checkerboards.

5. Paint the wheels and handle Gloss Black using a brush. Paint trim colors of your choice.

Glass painting was a popular folk art in early Europe which was brought to America by immigrants in the 17th century.

Brilliant and elegant, decorative glass has become one of the most desirable painting surfaces.

Painting on glass has become much easier and more convenient because paints are now permanent and available in a wide variety of colors.

Decorating dinnerware, pretty perfume bottles, or romantic candleholders, can be a very satisfying form of creative expression.

This charming plate is ringed with bright cherries surrounding a blue checkerboard design... ready for a piece of pie or a summer fruit salad. (page 69)

A·I·N·T·I·N·G

Enliven summer luncheons with brightly painted glassware adorned with colorful fruits, flowers, checkerboards and dots (at left and lower left).
(page 68)

Set the table for a romantic dinner with lacy-trimmed goblets and plates. The tiny vase, painted to match, is ready for a small bouquet of flowers.
(page 67)

A soft, pink rose motif adds feminine charm to the heart-shaped perfume bottle, votive candleholder and two floral vases. Imagine any of these attractive pieces gracing a pretty dressing table.

(page 71)

Warm, glowing candlelight from a star-studded hurricane lamp and candleholder enhances the sophisticated celestial designs painted on glassware for an elegant holiday dinner party. Gold paint and deep-hued, royal purple add glamour (at left).

(page 70)

Years ago, glass was a difficult surface on which to paint, but now with new and improved paints, it's fun, easy, and foolproof.

Searching for the glassware is half the fun. You can find paintable glass in department stores, craft, and discount stores. Other glass items can be found at garage sales, flea markets and second hand stores. Keep your eyes open for clear dishes, candleholders, vases, goblets, glasses, bowls, etc. You'll be surprised how magically you can transform a plain glass item into an exquisite heirloom piece.

Supplies:
Glass paints
Surface Conditioner
Good set of brushes - angulars, shaders, liners, rounds and flats
Paper towels
Container for water
Palette for mixing paint
Cotton swabs
Craft knife
Tracing paper and pencil

Un-do (adhesive remover) handy for removing price stickers or labels from glass items)
The paint used in this chapter is Delta Air-Dry PermEnamel. It's dishwasher, oven and microwave-safe. The paint can be mixed to create new colors and cleans up with soap and water.

General instructions:

1. Remove any labels or stickers using Un-do.

2. Wash the item with soap and water.

3. To transfer the design: trace the design from the book with tracing paper and pencil.

4. Tape the pattern to the inside of glass. If the item is rounded, press it in place and smooth it out. Use the pattern as a guide and paint on top of the glass over the pattern. If this isn't possible, just look at the patterns and freehand the design.

5. Brush on the surface conditioner with a clean, dry brush (this is the most important step - the conditioner bonds the paint to the glass). Let it dry. Do not rinse off or wipe off.

6. Apply paint in the colors of your choice with a clean, dry brush. Do not thin with water.

7. Let each application dry before applying the next color. If you make a mistake, use a cotton swab to wipe it off immediately before it dries. If paint has dried and you wish to change something, simply scrape off the paint carefully with a craft knife. Then reapply the paint.

8. After the paint dries, brush with Clear Gloss Glaze. The glaze should be applied over the painted design, not over the entire glass.

Note - To be extra safe, it's better if the paint is only applied to the areas of the glassware that don't come into direct contact with food or drink. The goblets pictured in this chapter are purely decorative and not intended for drinking. If you plan to drink from your goblets, paint the design 1/4" down from the rim.

FRUIT COLLECTION
Pictured on page 64

Paint - Red Red, Dusty Pink, White, Black, Crocus Yellow, Light Blue, Tangerine, Mulberry, Apple Candy Green, Hunter Green
Brushes - #1 round, #4, #6 and #8 shaders

Rose Bud Vase
(Syndicate Sales)
Pictured on page 64

1. Paint circular roses Red Red with a #4 shader and the inner swirl Pink, with a #1 round.

2. Paint leaves Hunter Green with a #1 round.

3. Paint White border at top of vase with a #8 shader and then Black checks.

4. Dot in between roses with Crocus Yellow using end of small brush.

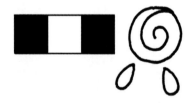

Floral Salt and Pepper Shakers
Pictured on page 64

1. Dot center of flowers with Crocus Yellow and flower with Red Red. (Reverse colors of flowers on other shaker).

2. Paint small scallops around top of shaker in Light Blue with a #4 shader.

Fruit Bowl
(Syndicate Sales)
Pictured on page 64

1. Paint upper and lower edges with a 3/8" wide band of White using a #8 shader. Paint Black checks using #8 shader.

2. Paint a piece of fruit on each section of bowl. Paint cherries in same colors and manner as Cherry plate (Pg. 64)

3. Paint body of orange slice Crocus Yellow with a #6 shader. Paint rind and inner sections Tangerine (use a small round to outline and a #3 shader to fill in). Dot small berries Mulberry. Paint stems Apple Candy Green with #1 round.

4. Detail stem of fruit bowl with Black dots.

DAISY COLLECTION
Paint - White, Black, Red Red, Dusty Pink, Hunter Green, Crocus Yellow, Deep Coral, Tropical Purple, Mulberry
Brushes - #4, #8 shader, #1, #5 round, liner

Salt and Pepper Shakers
Pictured on page 64

1. Paint bottom edge of shaker White with a #8 shader. Paint every other check Black.

2. Dot one shaker Black and the other White.

Roses and Daisy Vase
(Syndicate Sales)
Pictured on page 64

1. Paint roses around top opening Red Red with #4 shader. Paint Dusty Pink swirl in each center using a #1 round brush.

2. Paint leaves Hunter Green with #1 round brush.

3. Paint daisies around bottom of vase Crocus Yellow with a #1 round. Dot the centers Red Red. Paint leaves in Hunter Green with #1 round.

4. Paint Black and White checks around top and bottom neck of vase with #8 shader.

5. Dot neck of vase Red Red.

Small Floral Vase
(Syndicate Sales)
Pictured on page 64

1. Paint top of vase Crocus Yellow with #8 shader. When dry, paint stripes Tropical Purple with a #5 round.

2. Paint the next stripe Deep Coral.

3. Paint the flowers Deep Coral, Tropical Purple and Mulberry and the centers of the flowers Crocus Yellow with a #1 round. Paint the leaves Apple Candy Green with the #1 round, the tendrils with a liner.

Cherry Plate
(Beacon)
Pictured on page 64

10" glass plate
Paint - Light Blue, White, Red Red, Apple Candy Green, Black Accent Liner
Brushes - 1/2" flat, #1 round, #4 and #6 shader

Cherry pattern at left. Checker pattern on page 71.

1. Paint checks Light Blue with a 1/2" flat. (Paint underside of plate)

2. Cherries - paint White highlight on cherries with a comma stroke with a #1 round.

3. Fill in cherries with Red Red using a #6 shader. Paint leaves Apple Candy Green. Paint stems with a Black Accent Liner.

4. Dot between cherries in Black.

LAVENDER AND LACE COLLECTION

Pictured on page 65
Pattern on page 71

Paint - Tropical Purple, White
Brushes - #6, #8 shader, 1/2" flat

Goblets

Pictured on page 65

1. Paint lace around rim in Tropical Purple using pattern and a #6 shader (1/4" flat).

2. Paint around base of goblet stem with White using a #10 shader (3/8" flat). Paint Tropical Purple checks with same brush.

3. Using the end of a large brush, dot centers of each lace scallop White. Dot around scallops in White using the end of a small brush.

4. Using the end of a large brush, dot around body of goblet in Tropical Purple.

Lavender & Lace Plate - 10"

(Beacon)
Pictured on page 65

1. Paint scallops in same manner as goblets.

2. Paint checks around inside circle of plate.

3. Dot center of plate with Tropical Purple using the end of a large brush.

Sweetheart Vase

(Syndicate Sales)
Pictured on page 65

1. Paint scallop around top opening of vase. Add detail dots on scallops with White.

2. Paint around bottom section of vase in White. Paint 1/2" Tropical Purple stripes using a 1/2" flat.

3. Dot around body of vase in Tropical Purple. Dot around top edge with White.

CELESTIAL COLLECTION

Pictured on page 66

Paint - Royal Purple, Gold Accent Liner
Brushes - #1 flat, #4 and #8 shader, #5 round

Celestial Plate - 10"

(Beacon)
Pictured on page 66

1. Paint outside rim of plate Royal Purple (2 coats) with #8 shader, paint around stars and moons leaving them clear. (Paint on underside of plate)

2. Using a Gold Accent Liner, paint around inside circle of plate along edge of purple.

3. Paint stars in center of plate by intersecting three lines using a Gold Accent Liner.

Celestial Goblets

Pictured on page 66

1. With #8 shader, paint 1 1/2" wide band of Royal Purple (2 coats) around goblet, painting around moon and stars, leaving them clear.

2. Paint a line around bottom edge of purple using a Gold Accent Liner.

3. Paint stars around body of glass in same manner as plate.

4. Paint around base of glass stem in Royal Purple with a #8 shader (3/8" flat). Paint lines toward the center stem using Gold Accent Liner.

Celestial Candleholder

(Mangelsen's)
Pictured on page 66

This candleholder is made up of different shaped sections. Paint some sections Royal Purple with a #4 shader, while leaving others clear.

Accent facets or shapes with Gold Accent Liner. Paint stars or the base in the same manner as goblets and plate.

Hurricane Lamp

(Mangelsen's)
Pictured on page 65

1. Paint a 2" wide band of Royal Purple at top and bottom edge of lamp (2 coats) with a 1" flat brush.

2. Paint a line around edges of purple with Gold Accent Liner. Detail purple band with Gold stars.

3. Paint gold swirls with #5 round in main body of lamp using pattern as guide.

ROMANTIC ROSE COLLECTION

Pictured on page 67

Paint - Dusty Pink, Mulberry, Hunter Green, Seafoam Green , White Frost (for etched glass look).
Brushes - #4, #8 shader, 3/4" flat, liner, #1 round
Sponge

Votive Candleholder

(Mangelsen's)
Rose Bowl (Syndicate Sales)

Pictured on page 67

1. Paint loose roses in Dusty Pink with a #8 shader brush. While still wet, loosely paint darker accents in Mulberry.

2. Paint base of leaf in two strokes of Hunter Green with a #8 shader. Paint in a highlight with one stroke of Seafoam Green.

3. Add little dots of Dusty Pink using the end of a small brush.

4. Paint in Hunter Green tendrils with a liner.

Floral Cylinder
(Syndicate Sales)
Pictured on page 67

1. Paint 3/4" wide Seafoam vertical stripes around cylinder with a 3/4" flat brush. (Use tape if desired.)

2. Paint roses in same manner as Votive and Rose Bowl.

Rose Heart Bottle
Pictured on page 67

1. Paint circular roses in Dusty Pink with #4 shader.

2. Dot center of roses in Mulberry. Dot around roses in a few places with Dusty Pink.

3. Paint two comma strokes of Mulberry in each rose using a #1 round.

4. Paint Hunter Green leaves with a #1 round.

5. Sponge over entire bottle with White Frost for an etched glass look.

6. Paint cork Dusty Pink.

American tole painting traces its origins to rosemaling, a style of folk art popular in Norway. Early American tinsmiths adapted these designs as embellishments for kitchen utensils. Originally labeled "tole", these items referred to a type of enameled metalware.

Tole painting has evolved to include some of the same designs and brush strokes. Examples of this art form include the antique chair embellished with roses and the sampler chest, a lesson in popular brush strokes.

Kitchen accessories come alive with the addition of tole painted fresh vegetables. Bright red radishes, orange carrots and glossy green peas embellish a black and white ground for cheerful results. A welcoming floorcloth, silverware caddie, and flower pot extend the design. Disguised as a kitchen catch-all, this cleverly painted ice cream carton can store cooking accessories, coupons or napkins. (page 81)

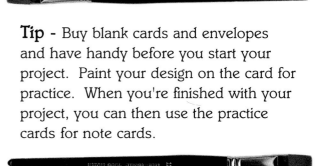

Tip - Buy blank cards and envelopes and have handy before you start your project. Paint your design on the card for practice. When you're finished with your project, you can then use the practice cards for note cards.

Paint this Northwest design on a floorcloth and country clock to decorate a mountain cabin or masculine retreat. (page 82)

Luscious roses and a folk art checkerboard change a simple treasure box into a family heirloom (at left).

Four different pastel designs painted on the drawers of this sampler chest are perfect for practicing brush strokes (bottom left).

This small antique chair modified to hold a flowering plant, is colorfully painted with pink roses and flowing ribbons (below).

(All on page 84)

Adapt an artistic impression of an English country cottage to a functional coat rack. The floral border becomes the centerpiece on a matching chair. Soft pastels and lightly sponged paint add to the aged appearance.
(page 84)

Tole painting has evolved today to include designs and brush strokes brought to this country by early folk painters.

One of the really fun things about tole painting is searching for painting surfaces (old antique wooden pieces or new unfinished wood items). As you poke through garage sales, flea markets or just around your house, you'll find yourself looking at things in a new light.

In this chapter some old pieces, new pieces, floor cloths and even an ice cream carton have been painted. Have fun finding your "new treasures".

Some things you should know before you start painting:

Brushes - buy the very best brushes you can afford. You'll be happy you did and your work will show it. For this type of painting, use synthetic brushes.

Care of brushes - When you buy a new brush, you should remove the sizing first - rub the hairs between your fingers, then clean the brush in water. Allow to dry completely before starting to paint.

After you finish painting, wash the brush using a brush cleaner. There are several good ones on the market. Apply the cleaner to the bristles and work it in with your fingers. Rinse with water. Dry the bristles on a paper towel or soft cloth and reshape the bristles.

Never let paint dry in your brush. Never let brushes soak in water.

Brush types

Flat - for stroking and blending

Round - for lines and small details

Mediums - gels or liquids that are used with paint to achieve different effects.

Floating medium -used in place of water for side loading.

Blending Gels - helps to make blending paints easier.

Extenders - acrylic paints dry very quickly. Extenders mixed with the paint increases the drying time. It also helps to create transparent to opaque effects.

Varnishes - used to protect your piece and applied after painting with a soft, flat brush. Available in matte, satin and gloss finishes.

Tack cloth - a piece of cheesecloth or soft cloth that's been treated with a mixture of varnish and linseed oil. It's used to clean pieces after sanding.

Wood preparation

Old wood: Clean with a wax-free cleaner and sand the design area lightly before applying pattern.

New wood: Fill all nail holes with wood putty as directed on container. Sand wood. Clean with tack cloth and base coat with the base color of your choice.

Applying the pattern - Make a tracing of your pattern and position it on your piece. Tape it in a few places, slip graphite paper under it (shiny-side down) and trace the design onto the piece. Never use carbon paper.

The strokes

A few basic strokes have been used to paint the designs in this chapter. Practice these strokes before beginning and when you feel comfortable with your results, you can then start painting your chosen project.

LOADING THE BRUSH

Full Loading - Flat Brush
Touch the brush into the puddle of paint at a 45 degree angle. Touch into paint then pull away from the puddle. Load all the way across the chisel edge of the brush. Try not to apply too much pressure when loading. Load no more than 3/4 of the way up the fibers.

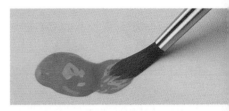

Full Loading - Round Brush
Touch brush into the puddle and pull away gently. Brush is at a lower angle to load. Paint can go all the way up to the ferrule on the round brush.

Sideloading - Flat Brush
Dampen your brush with water or Extender. Then touch one side into the paint on palette. Place the corner of your brush on top of pulled-down paint and pull gently away. Repeat until there is the desired color on one side of brush and dissipating color toward the opposite side.

iner Brush

hin the paint by dipping the rush into water or Extender. oad with paint up to the ferrule. ull and twist gently away from he puddle.

ouble Loading - Flat Brush

ull load first color onto brush. hen side load the second color. ontinue to gently pull paint way from the puddle in the ame spot to completely blend he dark and light values, eating a middle value.

BRUSH STROKES
Flat Brush Strokes
"C" Stroke

Touch chisel edge of brush to the surface.

Pull brush on a curve. On the downward pull, apply pressure to create width for the "C".

End up at the bottom of the "C" with the brush perpendicular to the surface and drag the line parallel to the top of the "C".

"C" Stroke (Reverse)

This is done in the same way, but curving the brush in the opposite way.

S" Stroke

Touch the chisel edge of the brush to the surface and pull toward the left.

Apply pressure on the downward pull. Slightly curve down to the left and back to the right.

End up on the chisel edge of the brush, pulling towards left again. The brush should be perpendicular to the surface.

"U" Stroke

Starting on the chisel edge of brush, push or pull in desired direction. Apply pressure for the amount of time needed to create the proper width.

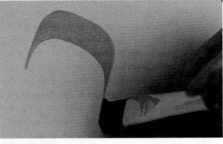

Pull back up onto the chisel edge to finish opposite side of the "U".

Modified "U" Stroke

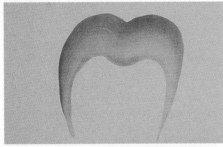

Start with the chisel edge held perpendicular to surface.

As you pull through the length of the scroll, gradually flatten your brush to its full width. Dip the center by increasing pressure.

End by lifting off the surface on the chisel edge.

Leaf #1

Make a modified "S" stroke. Beginning at bottom and pulling up to chisel edge.

Make a mirror image stroke, beginning at top on chisel edge and pulling down to broad edge. Close bottom with slight pivot.

ROUND BRUSH STROKES

Vertical Comma

The size of brush and the amount of pressure determines the size of the stroke. Fully load brush with paint all the way to the ferrule. A good comma stroke has a rounded head and diminishing tail.

Touch tip to surface; allow hairs to spread to desired size. Pull brush toward you to create the tail.

Gradually release pressure, coming up on tip of brush, as you finish your stroke. Also, slightly twist the brush in your fingers to gather the hairs together. The brush is perpendicular to the surface at the end.

Left and Right commas

Load as for the vertical comma. Touch the surface with pressure. Push to the left or the right as you drag and lift the brush. Then pull in the opposite direction as you gradually lift the brush from the surface.

Twist brush as for vertical comma to end stroke with a nic diminishing point.

"WELCOME TO MY KITCHEN" COLLECTION

Paint (Delta Ceramcoat)
White, Pale Yellow, Tangerine, Bright Red, Lime Green, Black
Brushes - #6 & #10 flat, #0 Script Liner, Large flat brush for varnishing
Water-based varnish

Welcome to My Kitchen Floorcloth

Pictured on page 74

Floorcloth, pre-primed, 18"x30"
(Tara Materials, Inc.)

1. Enlarge pattern (page 88) 200%. Trace the design onto the floorcloth using graphite paper.

Painting: As you follow instructions for painting each area, look at the color photo for line, shading and highlighting placement.

2. Background and checks: White areas are pre-painted on prepared rugs. Paint Black areas, dry and with liner brush paint a White line between checks and Black background of vegetable area. Paint a Black line between checks and White background of center area. Paint the edges of cloth Black and White to match checks.

3. Lettering: Paint letters Bright Red to cover, drying between coats. Line letters with liner brush in Black.

4. Vegetables: Paint all green areas, peas, leaves, and stems, Lime Green.

5. Peas: Highlight leaves, pods and peas with a side load of Pale Yellow. Line inside of pods, veins, and around caps with liner in Black.

6. Carrots: Base carrots in White, then paint Tangerine to cover. With a liner brush, pull in lines of Black. Highlight carrot tops by painting C strokes, top down, with a side loaded brush of Pale Yellow.

7. Cherries: Base cherries in White. Paint Bright Red to cover. Highlight by painting a C stroke, on the left side of each cherry, with a side loaded brush of Pale Yellow. Shade along inside of leaves with a side load of Black. Paint inside edge of leaves with a Black line and highlight along left side of that line with a side load of Pale Yellow.

8. Dots: With the wooden end of your brush, dip into fresh White paint and dot onto cloth. Use fresh paint for each dot.

9. Finish: When paint is completely dry, finish with two to three coats water-based varnish.

Clean the floorcloth with a damp rag and warm, soapy water.

Silverware Caddie and Fruit and Vegetable Box

Pictured on page 74

Wooden Caddie
Ice Cream Carton
(Patterns at bottom of page)

1. Basecoat in Black.

2. With white graphite paper, trace the fruit and vegetable designs randomly on the pieces.

3. Paint using directions for the floorcloth.

4. Dot with White paint

5. Paint White checkerboard stripes on the edge of the caddie and top lid of the carton.

5. Seal with varnish.

Flower Pot

Pictured on page 74

6" clay pot
Paint - Black and White
Brush - 1" sponge brush

1. With sponge brush, paint the pot Black. You may need 2 coats.

2. With flat brush, paint 2" White stripes on the rim of pot.

3. With the end of the brush, dip into White paint and dot randomly on the sides of the pot.

4. Apply varnish of your choice.

LODGE COLLECTION
Pictured on page 75

Paint (Delta Ceramcoat)
   Navy Blue, Ocean Reef
   Blue, Hunter Green,
   Palomino Tan, Cardinal
   Red, White, Black
Graphite Paper - white and black

Reindeer Clock
Pictured on page 75
(pattern at right)

Wooden Clock (Walnut Hollow)

Reindeer Floorcloth
Pictured on page 75

Pre-primed floorcloth (Tara Materials, Inc.)

1. Basecoat the clock in Navy Blue, blending up to Ocean Reef Blue at the top.

2. Trace on the design using white graphite paper for the clock and black for the floorcloth. (Pattern for floorcloth, page 86.)

3. Paint the trees Hunter Green, pulling comma strokes (White mixed with a little Green) at the edge of the branches.

4. Trace the reindeer, ground and triangle design at the bottom of the trees.

5. Paint the reindeer and ground Palomino Tan, the triangles Red. On the floorcloth, paint the checkerboard Black and White.

6. Paint the White snow dots using the end of the brush dipped in White paint.

7. Paint the base of the clock Palomino Tan. Paint the bottom edge Black and White checkerboard with a 1/4" wide flat brush.

8. Paint the ball feet Red.

9. Paint around the inside curved edge of the clock Red, the outer edge, Black.

10. Seal with varnish, 3 coats for floorcloth.

ROSE COLLECTION
Pictured on page 77

All of the following designs use this paint palette:

(Delta Ceramcoat) White, Ivory, Custard, Straw, Raw Sienna, Native Flesh, Wild Rose, Purple Dusk, Raspberry, Tangerine, Blue Mist, Periwinkle Blue, Denim Blue, Copen Blue, Paynes Grey, Green Sea, Lime Green, Pine Green

Brushes - #2, 4, 6 and 8 flat
    #3 round
    #1 liner

A large, flat for varnishing and large and small scuzzy brushes (an old flat brush with the bristles well spread out).
You will also need:
Tracing and graphite paper
Tack cloth

Paint the following designs using the general stroke instructions below:

Leaf #2 - Load a flat brush in Green Sea and side load in Pine Green. Pull a modified S stroke with the Pine Green to the top. Load brush in Green Sea and pull a C stroke to meet up with the S stroke.

With liner brush, paint a comma stroke of Pine Green in the center. For leaves with liner work, load liner brush and pick up a tiny scoop of paint on its tip. Paint from just past the tip of the leaf up around the S stroke. Then line around edge of C and the lower part of the leaf tip. Keep liner work loose and casual.

Buds

Fingertip Rose: Put out a small puddle of Wild Rose. Touch your little finger into this puddle and lightly tap off excess on palette then gently place loaded finger onto your wood piece. With a liner brush loaded in White, paint two tiny comma strokes, one above the other, following the shape of your finger print. Put one White dot at the top of the bud.

Simple Rose Bud: Load a #4 flat brush in Wild Rose, side load in White and blend. With the White toward the top of your brush, pull an inverted U stroke.

Reload your brush and, with the White to the top, pull a regular U stroke making sure that this stroke covers the bottom of the first stroke.

Blue Bud: Load a small flat brush in Periwinkle blue and side load in White. Paint the same as the simple bud.

Flowers

Simple Rose: Load a #8 flat brush in Wild Rose; side load one side in White, the other in Raspberry and blend. With the White to the top or outside, pull C or U strokes following the shape of your petals. Reload your brush and pull an inverted U stroke at the top of the bowl of the rose making sure to cover the bottom of the top petals.

Load again and with the White to the top, pull a regular U stroke making sure to cover the bottom of your inverted U. These two strokes will form the cup of your rose.

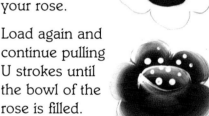

Load again and continue pulling U strokes until the bowl of the rose is filled. Scatter dots of White in the cup of your rose.

Fluffy Rose:

Base color #1 - Native Flesh
Base color #2 - Native Flesh plus Wild Rose

Load a #8 brush in #1 or for a pinker rose - #2. Side load in White and tip the corner of your brush in White. Paint petals with ruffled U strokes allowing brush to wiggle up and down as you paint. Reload as needed so your paint is fresh and your White stays strong.

Load a #8 brush in #1 or #2 and base in the bowl of your rose with shape-following strokes then reload in base color, side load in White, tip in White and pull the strokes on the top of the rose with ruffled inverted U strokes.

Mix Raspberry and Purple Dusk and with a scuzzy brush, tap into the cup area of the rose and on the petals next to and around the bowl of your rose. Reload

your flat brush in #1 or #2 color, side load and tip in White and paint petals over the bowl of the rose with ruffled U strokes.

Daisy #1 - Load a #1 round brush or liner brush in Custard and tip it into White. Paint comma stroke petals, starting at the tip of the petal and pulling toward the center. Paint tiny White comma strokes here and there between and over the petals. With a flat brush, paint center in Raw Sienna, dry and with a scuzzy brush lightly tap with Raspberry plus Purple Dusk.

Daisy #2 - Paint as #1 except after basing center Raw Sienna, loosely dot Straw onto bottom half of the center and Wild Rose on the top half. Let these dots splash out over petals.

Daisy Bud - Base bud area in Custard, dry and paint comma strokes from top to bottom with a liner brush loaded in Custard

and tipped in White. For stem paint Green comma strokes.

Lilac Puffs - Load a scuzzy brush in Purple Dusk and lightly pounce into flower shape. Without cleaning brush, tap into White and pounce onto Purple mostly on one side but be loose about this.

Blue Fill Flowers - Load a #2 flat brush in Periwinkle Blue and tip one corner in White then pull tiny C strokes following petal lines. Dot in centers of Custard and a tiny drop of Deep Green.

Rose Box
Pictured on page 76

1. Basecoat Ivory and dry.

2. Wrap a small piece of terry toweling around your fingers and tap into Native Flesh. Tap off excess paint and then softly tap color along the bottom and sides of the top of the lid covering more of the lid under where flowers will go (see photo). With toweling, softly tap in a little Periwinkle blue, then Raw Sienna and then White until you have achieved the look you like. While your lid is drying, tap the same colors onto the sides of the box. With the #8 flat brush, paint the checks Periwinkle Blue.

Paint the Design:
(See photo pages 73 & 76)

Leaves: See directions, Leaf #2.

Roses: See directions, fluffy roses

Daisies: Follow directions for Daisy #1 and Daisy Bud.

Finish: Add loose liner strokes of Green Sea plus Straw and random tear drops of Native Flesh. Dry and terry sponge lightly over the design with white. Dry and varnish.

Sampler Chest of Drawers
Pictured on page 76

1. Basecoat chest in Custard

2. Base one drawer White, one Blue Mist, one Custard and one White plus Wild Rose. Base knobs White.

3. Dot fingertip roses on sides of the chest, on the Custard drawer and on each knob.

4. Paint comma leaves Green Sea on either side of each rose.

5. Dot Blue drawer in White.

6. On the Pink drawer - paint leaves with Green Sea, lines in Pine Green. Dot with custard. (pattern page 85)

7. Paint plaid on Blue drawer with a flat brush and Periwinkle Blue, lining in Denim Blue.

8. Paint checks in Denim Blue.

9. Dry and sand Pink drawer and Blue drawer to give them an aged look.

10. Dry and varnish.

Planter Chair
Pictured on page 76

Antique planter chair (A Place in the Garden)
Plant that fits in chair
(pattern page 91)

1. Painting from back to front, paint in leaf #1 with lines, simple roses and simple rosebuds and lilac puffs.

2. Load a #8 flat brush in Wild Rose, tipping one side in White and the other in Raspberry, blend and paint extended S strokes for the ribbon. Load liner in Wild rose. Tip in Raspberry then in White and paint comma strokes. With terry rag, tap White lightly over roses.

Coat Rack

Pictured on page 76
(pattern page 90)

Wood coat or hat rack
Trace pattern - To begin, only
trace the arch shape and horizon
line (a midline between bush
area and sky).

Painting Scene:

1. Basecoat sky area in Blue
Mist being careful not to let paint
build up at horizon line.

2. Wrap a terry rag around your
fingers and tap into Denim Blue.
Tap off excess, then tap lightly
over the Blue Mist.

3. Wet a #8 brush in water, blot,
and sideload in White. Blend
once and form clouds with
loosely extended inverted U
strokes.

4. Dry and apply pattern for
house, trees and bushes.

5. Base house in Ivory, dry and
tap in heavy Ivory then heavy
White with scuzzy brush.

6. When house is dry, shade
under the eaves with a side load
of Brown Iron Oxide. Dry lightly,
tap with a terry rag over shaded
area and add more color if
needed.

7. Dry and apply pattern of
windows and doors.

8. With a flat brush, paint
windows Paynes Grey and door
Denim Blue. Dot light in
window with Custard and pull
tiny light lines away from dot.

9. Paint window trim Copen
Blue and shade front trim with a
touch of Paynes Grey.

10. Paint lines on door Paynes
Grey and highlight with lines of
Denim Blue plus White.

11. With a flat brush, base roof
in Straw plus Raw Sienna, dry
and with Raw Sienna dry-brush

over this and again, when dry,
dry-brush over with Straw.

12. Casually line with thinned
Black (See photo).

13. Base the chimney Wild
Rose, dry and shade with a side
load of Wild Rose plus Purple
Dusk.

14. Highlight with a side load of
White and paint in tiny random
horizontal lines to give the idea
of bricks.

15. Paint area under the house
in Sea Green plus Straw.

16. The trees and bushes are
formed by pouncing in color
with a scuzzy brush. First
pounce in Pine Green
then pounce in other
colors (Green Sea,
Green Sea plus Straw,
Pine Green plus Straw)
to show different
bushes and trees.
Pounce a bit of Paynes
Grey into the trees to
show depth. Be sure
not to pounce so
heavily that you lose
separation. Add in
scattered pounces of
Periwinkle Blue and
Denim Blue.

Painting Flowers -
Apply your flower and
leaf pattern then paint
leaves and flowers that
are the farthest back
first. Use leaf #1,
simple rose and daisy
#2 instructions.

Chair with Roses

Pictured on page 77
(pattern page 90)

Old or new chair with
large back area

1. Transfer on the
design and paint back
leaves and flowers

first. Follow the directions for
painted leaf #1 with liner, simple
roses, daisy #2, Blue fill flowers
and Lilac puffs and simple buds.

2. When all the work is dry, with
terry cloth wrapped around your
fingers, lightly tap some White
over flowers.

3. Dry and varnish.

4. For fluffy background, lightly
and loosely pounce in Raw
Sienna, Straw, White and Wild
Rose with a scuzzy brush,
keeping an oval shape in mind
or a shape that works with your
particular wood piece.

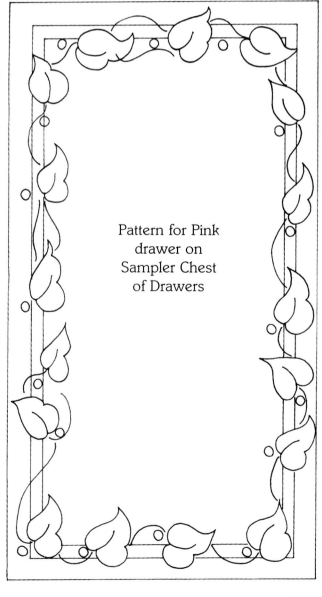

Pattern for Pink
drawer on
Sampler Chest
of Drawers

Enlarge 200%

Enlarge 200%

A · I · N · T · I · N · G

Painted and dyed fabrics are as old as the beginning of time. Early dyes were made of earth and plants and applied with crude tools.

Today, fabric paints and dyes are easy to use and come in a rainbow of colors.

To try this technique, paint a muted pastel floral pattern on a white, ruffled pillow, or bright, vibrant sunflowers on a pre-printed silk scarf.

With a little practice, fabric painting can enhance your home decor and fashions.

Tiny, delicate roses become the perfect counterpoint for shimmering, pastel beads on the shade of this boudoir lamp. A bouquet of painted roses, encircled by bead work, adorns a small pillow. Dramatic fringe adds a touch of elegance.

(page 99)

Tip- Save old pieces of fabric These can be used for practicing brush strokes and experimenting with types and colors of paints.

Make a pretty bed even more inviting by adding beautifully painted pillows. Paint one or paint them all to decorate your own Victorian setting.
(page 100)

A glorious sunflower becomes the pattern for this pre-printed silk fabric. Add fabric dyes to its luminescent surface for a gorgeous one-of-a-kind table topper or a fashionable scarf (left).
(page 101)

Painted silk, treated with salt creates a wonderfully magic effect. Tie the silk around a pillow form and finish with a knot. An easy expression of the ancient art of silk painting.
(page 101)

Painting on fabric can be fun and rewarding. All types of home decorating accessories can be created with a little paint, some imagination and inspiration.

An assortment of paints, good brushes and a surface to paint on are all you'll need to get started.

About fabric painting

Always remember to:

1. Prewash fabric and then press out wrinkles. (Do not prewash silk.)

2. Use natural fiber fabrics - cotton, cotton blends, silk, etc. Synthetic fabrics don't take the paint well and will fade after washing.

Methods for applying designs:

1. Transfer paper: Draw or trace the design on the paper and transfer to fabric.

2. Transfer pens: Trace the design using the transfer pen onto tracing vellum, then iron onto fabric.

3. Use a photocopy machine (dry toner type). Copy your design and use the photocopy to iron onto your fabric. The copy will be faint, but you can see it well enough to paint.

When ironing the design onto fabric, use "cotton" setting (for silk, use "silk" setting), NO STEAM, and a back and forth motion for about 10 - 15 seconds. Use a pressing cloth over your fabric.

Paints

There are many brands and types of paint available for fabric painting. The following information will help when

purchasing and using fabric paints.

Acrylic Paints - (usually available in 2 oz. bottles). Acrylic paints are very vivid in color, come in a huge selection of shades and clean up with soap and water. The paints will not penetrate the fabric and may feel stiff. Textile Medium should be added to help the paint penetrate and make the paint permanent.

With acrylics you will need to heat set your design. (Iron back of fabric for about 20 seconds or place in clothes dryer for 20 minutes.)

Fabric Paints - (available in 2 oz. bottles) There aren't quite as many colors to choose from, but the paints can be mixed for a wider palette. Fabric paints will penetrate better and you'll get a smoother and softer result. Design should be heat set (same as above). Clean up with soap and water.

Fabric Dyes - These are much thinner paints, almost as thin as ink. Fabric dyes are best used for silk painting or for dyeing fabrics such as in tie dyeing.

They penetrate into the fabric and have a smooth, soft feel.

Resist - (for silk painting) also called Gutta resist. This is used to outline your design. It forms a border which prevents the colors from spreading into each other.

There are other paints that work well on fabrics such as dimensional paints, and glitter paints. You may want to experiment with these alternative paints. It's a good idea to

practice on old pieces of fabric first before you actually paint on an expensive piece of fabric or pre-finished item.

Brushes

Use synthetic or animal hair brushes made specially for fabric painting. Inexpensive watercolor brushes are ideal for silk painting.

Caring for Fabric Painted Projects

Wash in washing machine on gentle cycle. Hand wash any delicate fabrics. Scotchguard items such as pillows that will receive a lot of use and may be difficult to launder (such as prefinished pillows with no opening). They can be cleaned off with a damp sponge.

Correcting Mistakes

Do not try to clean up a painting error, you will only smudge and spread the paint into the fabric. Instead, try to cover over your mistake by painting a new design element. This is where your creativity comes in!

Correcting mistakes when painting on silk

Always begin with light colors. If you make a mistake it's easier to cover it with another darker color. Use a Q-tip dipped in water or alcohol to correct errors, but be careful, it may leave a ring.

Romantic Rose Pillow

Pictured on page 94

Pillow - 7 1/2" square w/fringe
Ribbon - Pink - 1/2" wide x 12"
Paint - (Delta) Sachet Pink,
   Cactus Green,
Brush - #5 round
Transfer pen

(Beading Optional)
*Beads - size 14, light pink
   transparent, rose
   transparent, dusty rose,
   yellow transparent, gold
   metallic
Beading needle - size 13*

1. Transfer design to pillow (see pattern page 101). Follow manufacturer's instructions.

2. Paint rose design lines using Sachet Pink and Indiana Rose.

3. Paint leaves and S shape curves using Cactus Green.

4. Paint dot of Indiana Rose between S shape curves.

5. Add two yellow beads to center of a rose. Add two gold beads near center, then add two yellow beads next to gold. Stitch pink and rose beads over the painted pink area using 4 beads at a time.

6. Add rose bead to each dot.

7. At center of each rose, stitch three yellow beads and a circle of gold beads around them.

8. Cut two pieces of ribbon 6 inches long. Fold each in half and tack in position on stems (see photo).

9. Stitch three rows of gold beads where knot would be on bow.

Delicate Floral Lampshade

Pictured on page 94

Ecru lampshade edged
   with gimp
Paint - (Delta) Pink Frosting,
   Cactus Green
Brush - #5 round

(Beading optional)
*Beads - size 14, cream, light
green, light pink, pink
transparent, yellow transparent
Beading needle - Size 13*

1. Transfer design to lampshade, one section at a time (see pattern page 101).

2. Paint stem designs using Cactus Green. Paint leaves using tiny brush strokes next to stems. Paint petals Pink Frosting using tiny brush strokes

3. Using embroidery style beading needle, add 1 yellow bead to the center of each flower. Knot after each bead and start with newly knotted thread.

4. Bead fringe directly on bottom edge of gimp, Use single thread with knot on inside of gimp. Add on beads to create pattern (9 cream, 2 green, 5 pink transparent, 2 pink, 1 yellow, 1 pink, 5 pink transparent, 2 green, 9 cream) . Then add 1 green, 3 yellow, 1 pink, 3 yellow. Take the needle back through the last green bead in the opposite direction. Continue taking the needle back through all the remaining beads in that direction. Pull thread tightly. Yellow and pink beads at bottom will make a small loop.

5. Take the needle back through gimp and knot. Add another fringe by repeating this step on

every other thread loop on the gimp all around the shade.

All of the following projects were painted using Delta Ceramcoat acrylic paints. The brushes - #4 liner, #6 Flat Shader, #2 and #4 round.

Heart Pillow with Violet Bouquet

Pictured on page 95

Heart shaped pillow with ruffle
Paint - Pretty Pink, Lavender,
   Dark Forest, Pale Mint,
   Dark Jungle, Lavender,
   Purple, Moon Yellow.
Textile Medium (mix with paint)

1. Transfer design to center of pillow (see pattern page 103).

2. Paint as follows: Berries & Ribbon - Pretty Pink shaded with Lavender. Stems - Dark Forest. Leaves - Pale Mint shaded with Dark Jungle. Violets: Base - Lavender and Purple. Center - Moon Yellow

Ruffled Pillow with Ribbon Border and Violet Bouquet Center

Pictured on page 95

Prefinished pillow with ruffle
Paint - Periwinkle, Fjord Blue,
   White, Lavender, Pretty
   Pink, Flesh Tone, Phthalo
   Blue, Village Green, Dark
   Jungle, Island Coral,
   Rouge, Dolphin Gray,
Textile Medium (mix with paint)
Pattern on page 102 - 103

1. Transfer the ribbon design onto the pillowcase (see photo for placement).

2. Paint as follows: Large ribbon - Periwinkle shaded with Fjord Blue. Highlights - White. Violet

bouquet: Violets - Periwinkle mixed with Lavender with Lavender edges. Centers - Pretty pink. Edge of Center - Flesh Tone. Flower creases - Phthalo Blue. Stems & leaves - Village Green shaded with Dark Jungle. Small ribbon - Island Coral highlighted with White. Ribbon shadows - Rouge. Forget-Me-Knots - White shaded with Dolphin Gray.

Vine Border Pillow

Pictured on page 95

Rectangular pillow with lace
Paint - Dark Jungle, Leprechaun,
Textile Medium (mix with paint)
Pattern on page 101

1. Transfer leafy vine design to pillow arranging some of the design as a border and some in the center.

2. Paint as follows: Ivy - Dark Jungle shaded with Leprechaun. Stem - Leprechaun.

Pillowcase with Ribbon Border

Pictured on page 95

White pillowcase
Paint - Blue Heaven, Cape Cod,
    Ivory, White, Cadet Gray,
    Lilac, Purple, Phthalo Blue,
    Pretty Pink, Antique Gold,
    Flesh Tone, Lavender, Dark
    Jungle, Avocado

1. Transfer the design onto the pillowcase. (see photo for placement)

2. Paint as follows: Ribbon edging - Blue Heaven shaded with Cape Cod. Ribbon center - Ivory highlighted with white. Shadows at ribbon twist - Cadet Gray. Violets - Lilac shaded with

Purple and Phthalo Blue. Highlight with Pretty Pink. Violet Centers - Antique Gold and Flesh tone. Inside Ribbon Stripe - Lavender blended with White shaded with Lavender. Leaves and stem - Dark Jungle shaded with Avocado.

Rosebud Ruffled Pillow

Pictured on page 95

Prefinished pillow with ruffle
Paint - Antique Gold, Baby Pink,
    Lavender, Avocado,
    Leprechaun
Textile (mix with paint)
Pattern on page 101

1. Transfer rosebud designs randomly to pillow. (see photo)

2. Paint as follows: inside of bud, Antique Gold blended with Baby Pink and Lavender. Leaf and Stem - Avocado blended with Leprechaun.

Cherubs

Pictured on page 95

Rectangular flange type pillow
Paint - Dresden Flesh, Medium
    Flesh, Custard, Raw
    Sienna, Pretty Pink,
    Lavender, Blue Heaven,
    Cape Cod, Dark Jungle,
    Leaf Green, Dark Brown,
    Nightfall, Old Parchment
Textile Medium (mix with paint)
Pattern on page 102

1. Transfer cherub design to center of pillow.

2. Paint as follows: Cherub's bodies - Dresden Flesh with Medium Flesh shading. Hair - Custard shaded with Raw Sienna. Cherub outline - Raw Sienna. Wings - Pretty Pink shaded with Lavender. Highlight

with Blue Heaven. Ribbon - Blue Heaven. Ribbon shadow - Cape Cod. Foliage - Dark Jungle, Avocado, Leaf Green and Dark Brown for shading. Flowers - Cape Cod blended with Nightfall. Custard blended with Old Parchment. Pretty Pink blended with Lavender.

Rosebud Neck Roll Pillow

Pictured on page 95

Neck roll pillow with lace edge
Paint - Antique Gold, Pretty Pink,
    Lavender, Avocado,
    Leprechaun.
Textile Medium (mix with paint)
Pattern on page 102

1. Transfer design to each edge of the pillow.

2. Paint as follows: Inside bud - Antique Gold blended with Pretty Pink and Lavender; leaf & stem, Avocado blended with Leprechaun.

Sunflower Table Topper

Pictured on page 96

Silk Sunflower kit (Arty's)
SET5003
Everything is included in kit

1. Stretch the fabric using the Tri Fix frames included in the kit.
2. Start painting following the instructions in the kit. Just follow the lines as if you're coloring in a coloring book.

3. Set the color according to the manufacturer's instructions.

No-Sew Silk Splash Pillow

Pictured on page 97

White Silk Scarf - 32" square
12" Pillow form
Fabric dye (Pebeo) Yellow,
    Scarlet, Royal Blue,
    Green, Purple
Inexpensive water color brush
Coarse salt (can be Kosher, sea
    or pretzel salt.)

1. Cover work area with plastic.

2. Lay the scarf on the plastic.
No need to pin or tape.

3. Put a lot of dye in your
brush.

4. Paint big strokes of color in
arches all across the scarf. Let
the colors run together.

5. While the dye is still wet,
sprinkle with the coarse salt.

6. Let dry and brush off salt.

7. Set the color according to
manufacturer's instructions on
the fabric dye.

Silk Tip
To avoid a muddy
appearance, don't put
complementary colors
next to each other.
For instance - don't
put red next to green,
yellow next to purple
or blue next to orange.

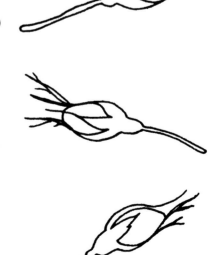

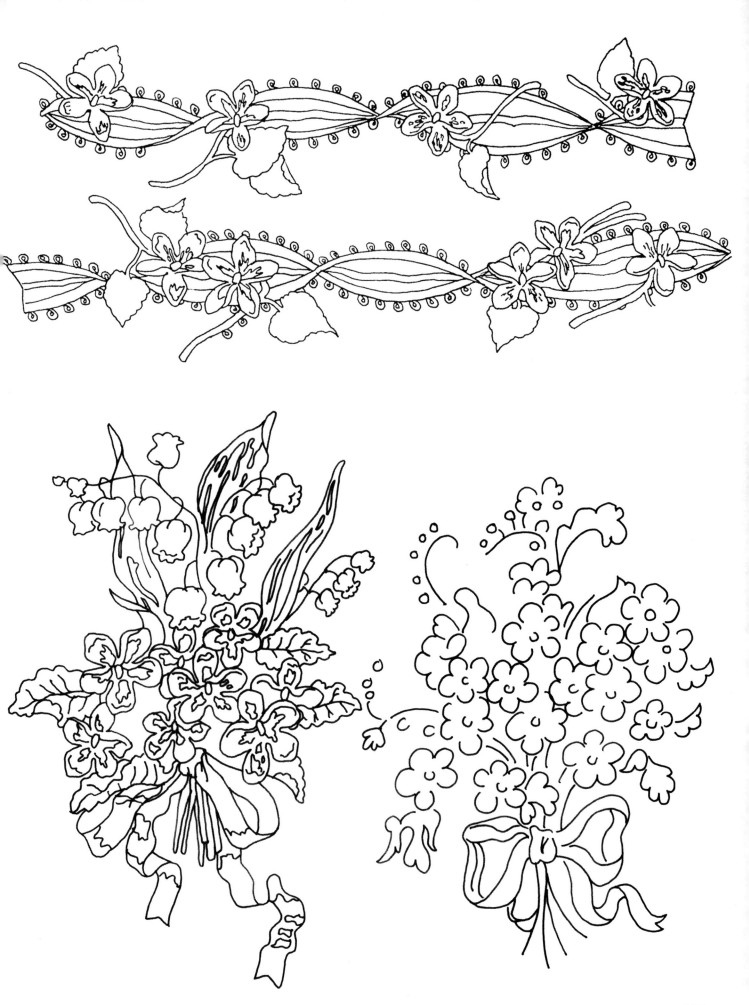

Oil painting is known as the medium of the masters. The rich and varied qualities of oils are typified by such diverse artists as Da Vinci, Rembrandt, and Van Gogh.

You're invited to try the step-by-step instructions for painting "Whitehall Cottage".

Once you've learned a few simple techniques, you will be able to paint your own special masterpiece.

Oil painting is an ideal technique for beginners because it is very forgiving. Corrections and changes can be made as you're going along by scraping away the wet paint.

These paints are versatile and can be used in a number of ways. There are no hard and fast rules with oil painting, just some general guidelines.

TECHNIQUE

Thin to Thick

One of the most common mistakes is painting too thickly and mixing up paints so that the colors get muddy. Learning how to apply the paint will prevent this from happening.

One way is to learn how paint is mixed on the canvas. This is done by painting thinly first - (dilute paint with turpentine). After painting the thin first shapes, you can then build up

your painting by using the thicker paint.

Dark to Light

Paint dark colors first and lightest colors last. The thickest paint should be for highlights.

Mixing a Color Pool

Mix up a pool of paint ranging from the darkest to the lightest shades of the color you are using. Mix colors loosely with a palette knife but be sure you can see each of the shades. Then as you paint, pick up a bit of the

...ure color on your brush and
...dd shades from your color
...ool.

Brushwork

Oil painting can be applied in
varying thicknesses which allows
the texture of the paint and the
brush strokes to play an
important part in the painting.

Descriptive brushwork -
following the direction of a form

Expressive - creating texture as
in Van Gogh's "Starry Night".

The type of brush strokes used
must be consistent throughout
the painting.

Impasto

Impasto is paint applied thickly.
This is mostly used for
highlighting an area. Some
artists use painting knives or
their fingers to build up the
texture. Paint is used up quickly
with this technique and can add
to your costs. To save money,
buy Impasto medium to thicken
your paint and make it go
farther.

Glazing

Glazing medium is added to
paint to thin it down and give it a
completely different look. It
becomes transparent and is
applied in a series of thin layers.
Glazing can be a tedious
technique because each layer
must dry before laying down the
next layer. But it's worth the
time because a rich and
luminous effect is achieved.

To save time, alternate layers
using some acrylics and then
oils.

Imprimatura

This term means laying a color
down on the canvas prior to
painting. It can be a thin layer.
The color you choose is
important. For beginners,
neutral shades are easiest to
work on such as browns,
ochres, or grays.

MATERIALS

Paints

Oil paints are a combination of
pigments bound with linseed oil.

They are more flexible than
acrylics as they don't dry as
quickly. You can move the color
around easily, mixing and
blending one wet color into
another.

When you start to paint with oils,
you must be careful not to lay
too many colors at once because
the colors will tend to get
muddy. This is easy to correct,
however. While the paints are
still wet, you can scrape off
muddy areas with a palette knife
and start again.

A good starter assortment of oils
would consist of:

Titanium White
Cadmium Yellow
Lemon Yellow
Yellow Ochre
Alizarin Crimson
Cadmium Red
Viridian (Green)
Raw Umber
Ultramarine
Cobalt Blue
Black
Buy the best oils you can afford.
It will be worth it.

Canvas

Fabric attached to a frame
(stretcher). Or you can also use
drawing or watercolor paper
which can be primed with a
layer of acrylic primer.

Brushes

Bristle brushes - #2, 6, & 8
rounds, flats and filberts
Soft sable brushes - #4 & 6
(to start out, use synthetic
brushes)

Painting Knife

Used for impasto effect and
creating texture. Can be used on
its edge to draw lines or sharp
edges. Or can be used on its
end to paint grasses, tree limbs
or rocks.

Palette Knife

Used to correct mistakes by
scraping paint off the canvas.

Mediums

Turpentine - for thinning paint

Linseed oil - for making paint
malleable

Palette

A wooden palette works best
(cure with linseed oil before
using).

Palette Cup

To hold medium and turpentine.
Fits on edge of palette.

Other supplies

Kneaded eraser
Sketch pad
Sketch box (to hold supplies)
Easel (can use sketch box as a
lap easel)

The Project

16"x 20" Canvas
Paints - Burnt Umber, Burnt Sienna, Veridian, White, Prussian Blue, Ultramarine Blue, Yellow Ochre, Cadmium Yellow Medium, Cadmium Red Light, Dioxazine Purple, Phthalo Green, Alizarin Crimson
Brushes - Sable or soft synthetic flats - #4, #6 and 1 inch, #3 round, #4 bristle
Graphite transfer paper
Pencil, Turpentine
Pattern on page 110

1. Transfer drawing to canvas with graphite paper. Trace over this with thinned Burnt Umber using a #3 round brush. Let dry. Thin the Burnt Umber even more and using a large brush, stroke over the whole canvas. Your drawing should show through.

2. Thin Veridian slightly and apply to trees and bushes, letting the brush strokes show. This should cover the underlying Burnt Umber drawing. Mix a fairly thin wash of: Phthalo Green, Yellow Ochre and White. Paint foreground. Mix Ultramarine, Yellow Ochre, White and a touch of Burnt Umber. Paint three fields with this. Paint distant hills a mixture of Prussian Blue, Burnt Umber and White. Paint the rest of the fields a mixture of Alizarin Crimson, White and a touch of Phthalo Green. This will be an undercoat. Paint hedgerows Burnt Umber and a touch of White and Violet. Paint the windows, thatched roof and door beam with this using a light quick stroke. Use this color for the shadows under the three bushes. Let dry.

3. Mix Yellow Ochre with touches of White and Burnt Umber, thin with a little turpentine and paint the roof. Let some of the darker color you have previously painted show through. Use a small, flat, fairly dry brush. Use short, quick strokes. Add a little more White and Yellow Ochre and touch in the higher spots above window.

Paint the shadow sides of the house with a pale mixture of White, Raw Umber and Blue.

Paint door Cadmium Red Light. Paint chimney Cadmium Red Light plus Burnt Sienna. Add white for the lighter side.

Paint over the pinkish fields with a mix of Cadmium Yellow Medium, Burnt Umber and a tiny dot of Phthalo green. Thin with turpentine.

1.

2.

Mix Raw Umber, Yellow Ochre, Phthalo Green, White, and work into tree tops. Use more on left and undersides, also some spots all over. Add more Phthalo Green to the mixture and paint the tops of the hedgerows. Let dry.

Mix Alizarin Crimson with a lot of white and dry-brush in the pink area in the middle foreground.

4. Paint the sky Ultra Blue mixed with White, blending from dark at the top to lighter at horizon. To soften the edge where it meets the hill, overlap slightly, then rub the overlap with a dry brush or rag.

Look at the finished painting on page 106 to complete the final details. Highlight hedgerows with Yellow Ochre.

Shade left sides of bushes around house with transparent mix of Phthalo Green and Prussian Blue with touch of Burnt Umber. Using the same color, with small round brush, make some thin broken lines on far left wall of cottage. the beginning of the hollyhocks.

Using all different shades of Light Green, add blades of grass using vertical strokes. Let dry.

Mix Prussian Blue, Ultramarine and white and dry brush over the Pink area. Make it look blurry and hazy.

Paint tree trunks mottled shades of Raw Umber and White. Shade left sides with a darker mixture.

Paint front of cottage White, going carefully around door and windows. With the point of the #3 round brush and thinned White paint, draw in the window panes. Don't try to make them perfect.

Put a touch of Yellow Ochre in White and glaze over door.

Mix White with a little Burnt Umber and turpentine, very pale and thin. Float this on top of far hill. If too White, blot it.

Add more greens to trees, darker, duller green under, lighter, brighter greens to tops. Add hints of Ultra Marine to tops.

Paint hollyhocks and foreground flowers White with tiny amounts of Alizarin Crimson with dark touches in center.

Add Light Ultramarine with a dry brush to the grass.

Add a little dioxazine Purple to Ultramarine and White and dry brush and dot into the flower field on the right.

5. Add any personal touches of your own and sign your painting.

3.

4.

Enlarge 200%

Paintings by contemporary artists whose work you might like to study for further ideas and inspiration.

Carol painted this landscape near a Southern California stream. The style is realistic with a fantasy feeling.

This painting was discovered in an antique store and is not signed. The anonymous artist had a wonderful feeling for expressing light.

Carol Bedolla

Richard Hagelberg

Richard's painting is an example of Representational Realism. Notice that the landscape is expressed without actually describing it. This was painted on location which is known as "Plein Air" painting.

W·A·T·E·R

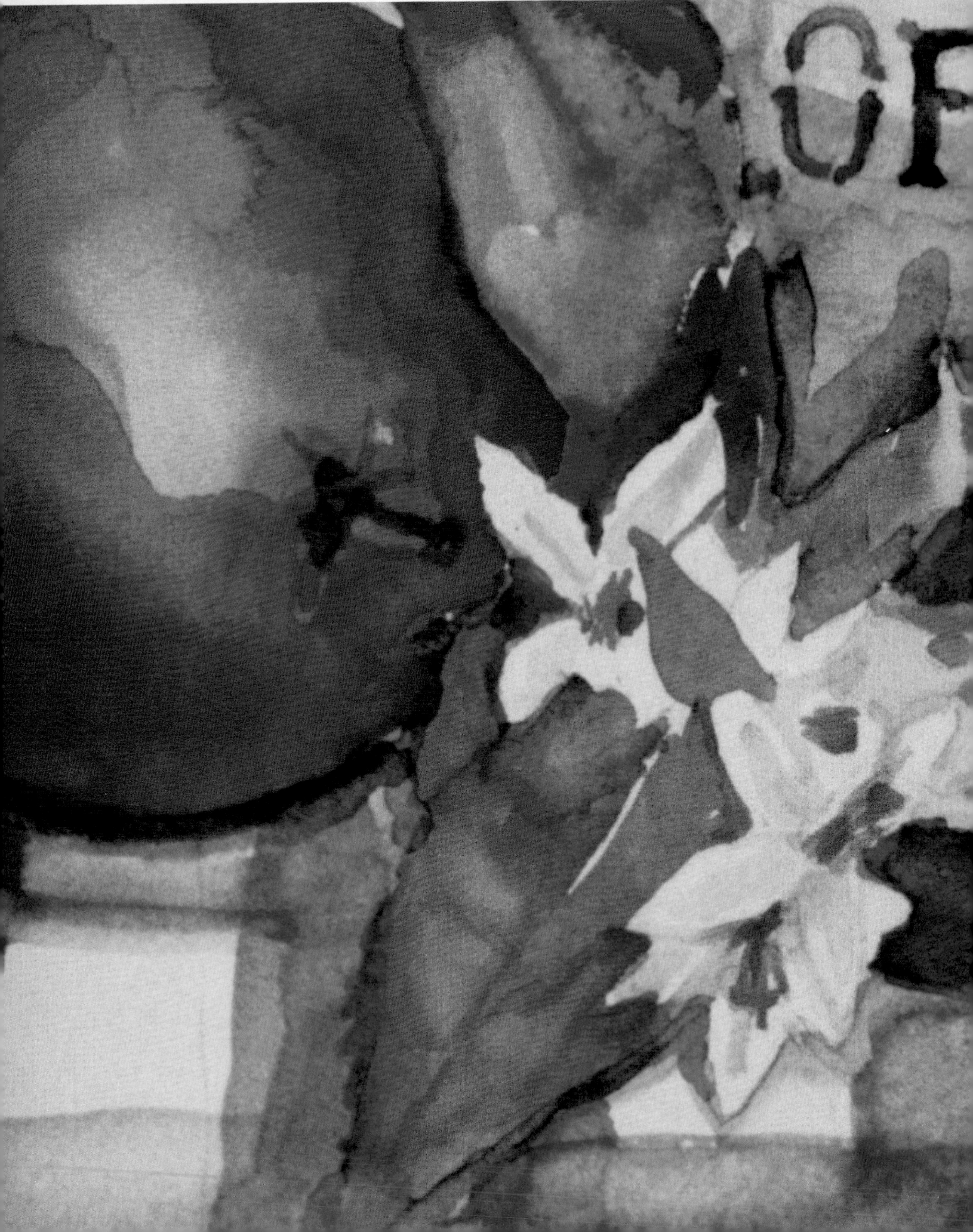

C·O·L·O·R

Watercolor is one of the oldest forms of painting. This technique evolved from the brushes of early Chinese artists to 18th century British painters.

The appeal of watercolors is obvious. Once you've experienced the fascinating spreading and blending of the colors across your paper, you'll be forever attracted to this medium.

Follow the step-by-step instructions to paint "Pa's Orange" and discover the satisfying techniques of watercolor.

Watercolor Technique
Two techniques are used for transparent watercolor:

1. Wet-On-Dry
The wet-on-dry technique requires the addition of layering colors or washes over paint that has dried. Deep colors are built up by adding one thin layer (wash) over another. Edges of dried layers are distinct.

Wet-on dry water color

a) dampen the entire blank painting surface with a sponge or brush.

b) Prop your painting surface at an angle to permit paint to flow from top to bottom.

c) Lay a flat, single color wash over the entire surface first.

d) Add a graduated wash, where color is darker at the top, or bottom of the surface.

2. Wet-On-Wet
The Wet-On-Wet technique requires the addition of colors mixed directly on the paper while the first color is wet. This results in subtle instant blending or fusing of colors. Edges of dried color are blurred.

Wet-on-wet water color
a) Control the flow of one color into another by tilting the painting surface.

b) Stop paint runs with a sponge or cotton ball to achieve different effects.

3) Add painting details when main areas of color are dry.

For paintings which contain both hard edges and soft color, use a combination of Wet-On-dry and Wet-On-Wet techniques.

Materials
Paint
Watercolor paint is sold in small tubes, pans and half pans. Tubes are the choice of most water color painters. Two qualities are available "artist's" and "students". Artist's quality, though more expensive, will yield better results with less frustration.

A good basic palette:
Yellow Ochre
Raw Umber
Viridian Green
Alizarin Crimson
Cerulean Blue
Payne's Gray
Lemon Yellow
Cadmium Yellow
Cadmium Red
French Ultramarine Blue
Moonglow (or Ultramarine Violet)

Paper
Water color paper is either machine-made or hand-made. Various types of both are available at art and craft supply stores.

Machine-made paper is least expensive and is often used by experienced painters.

a) cold pressed - a lightly textured paper popular for both washes and detailed work.

b) rough - a heavy textured paper which is difficult to use, but appropriate for some subjects.

c) hot pressed - a smooth finished paper. Can be frustrating for a beginner.

Pa's Orange

We recommend using a 140 1b. cold pressed as a beginning point. As you gain more experience, you can experiment with different types and weights of paper.

Brushes
A variety of brushes are designed for watercolor painting. They fall into two basic categories "round" and "flat". Each brush category is numbered by size. Other brushes are called riggers, filberts, hakes and larger rounds. An assortment of

O. Vice

brushes from #2 to #20 and flats from 1/2" to 2" are most used. Bristles can be synthetic or natural sable.

Palettes

White enameled, tin butcher's trays are popular as they permit accurate paint color mixing and can be cleaned easily. Any white, non-porous surface such as a ceramic plate is fine.

Tools

Common tools used by watercolor artists include: pencil, kneaded eraser, toothbrush, sponge, salt, paper towels, tissues and spray-type water bottles.

TIP - Always work on stretched paper. Pads of pre-stretched paper are available at art supply and craft stores.

The Project

You can paint! This step-by-step project is designed to introduce you to the world of watercolor. Let your inhibitions go, and try it!

Paint

Small tubes - (Daniel Smith paints were used) Cadmium Orange, Cadmium Red, Cobalt turquoise, Alizarin Crimson and Moonglow

Brushes - #10 or #12 round

Paper - 140 lb. machine-made, cold press paper (Montval by Canson was used for this project).

Other - Soft lead pencil, kneaded eraser, 2 containers clean water (one for cleaning brush), paper towels.

Procedure:

1. Set up your own "Orange Still Life" or use the pattern on page 118. To trace the pattern, hold the watercolor paper against a lighted window with the pattern under it and trace the design with pencil.

2. If you want to set up your own still life, place the orange in very bright light so that you'll be able to see range of lights and darks of the orange.

3. Using the pencil, draw the orange. Draw an interesting shape; not a perfect oval or round. Draw in the lightest areas (highlights).

4. When drawing the counter top, be sure to draw a continuous line lightly through the orange to make sure the counter line is level.

5. Dampen your entire brush in clean water container. Then, using a small amount of water on the brush, and a generous amount of Cadmium Orange, apply paint to bottom curved portion of the orange in a continuous stroke. Don't be afraid to use lots of paint. Colors fade as they dry.

6. Rinse your brush in water. Then brush on clean water alongside the already-painted edge. The paint will "bleed out" into the unpainted paper. Continue this process quickly across orange in curved sections, not straight.

7. Rinse brush again and continue this blending process, fading to the light area on top. Do not paint the white areas (highlights) that you've drawn in previously.

If your orange doesn't have enough changes in color you may wish to apply more Cadmium Orange to the base of the orange and then blend it in. Let this dry before going on.

5 - 7

8

8. Add Cadmium Red to brush and apply to the base of the orange. Use the same blending process as Step #5, but stop short of the light orange at top. This bright red will fade, so be sure to add enough color. This may seem too bright, but the brightness will fade when the background color is added.

9. Mix Cadmium Orange and Cobalt Turquoise to create green for the leaf and stem. Do not over-mix. The right side of the leaf will be light. Blend the leaf as you did the orange, applying full color to the left side. While leaf is slightly damp, drop a bit of Cadmium Orange to the top of the leaf. Then add Cobalt Turquoise to the left edge of the stem.

10. Apply a large amount of Cobalt Turquoise at lower right window. Fill in larger area. Add water to change intensity of turquoise. Use full color above the light area of orange and the lower left side. Use enough of water on your brush to spread the paint.

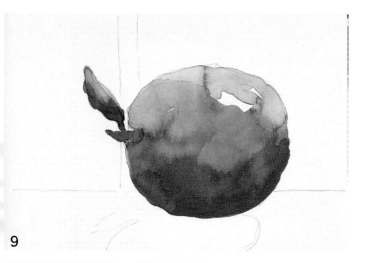

9

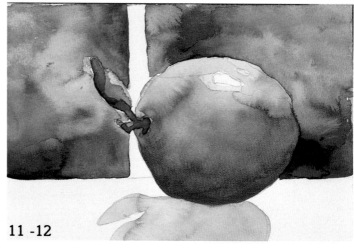

11 -12

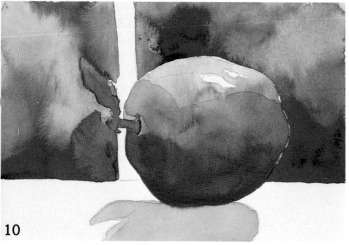

10

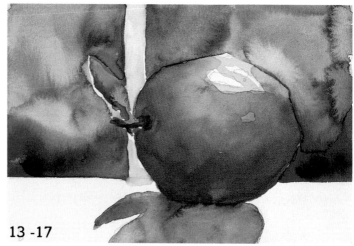

13 -17

11. Fill in the shadow with a light wash of Cobalt Turquoise. While Turquoise is still wet, drop in Cadmium orange in the left pane and right pane for reflected color in the window.

12. Drop in Alizarin Crimson to top and bottom of left pane and upper right side of window.

13. Add Moonglow to inside panes. Then use Moonglow to cover the turquoise shadow area of the orange.

14. Clean brush while shadow area is still damp. Then use a small amount of Cadmium Red to add the reflected color in the shadow of the orange and green to the left side of the shadow (color from leaf).

15. Mix a very small amount of Moonglow and Cadmium Red, then apply lightly over lower 1/3 of orange. Remember to keep strokes curved, not straight.

16. Add water to mixed Moonglow and Cadmium Red and apply to white pane behind orange.

17. Apply a line of Moonglow underneath the orange and let it slowly blend out and fade into the painted shadow area.

18. Sign your name and date your painting on the back. After doing many more paintings you can check your progress.

TIP- Squint your eyes often to see where light and dark area will appear. Your eyes work as hard as your hands in painting. Paint quickly, have fun and be delighted with your successes. If you have a desire for water color painting, continue exploring your creativity by taking classes.

Coffee, Gingham and Oranges

Odds and Ends

All paintings by Carilyn Vice

Tin Can Roses

A·C·R·Y·L·I·C·

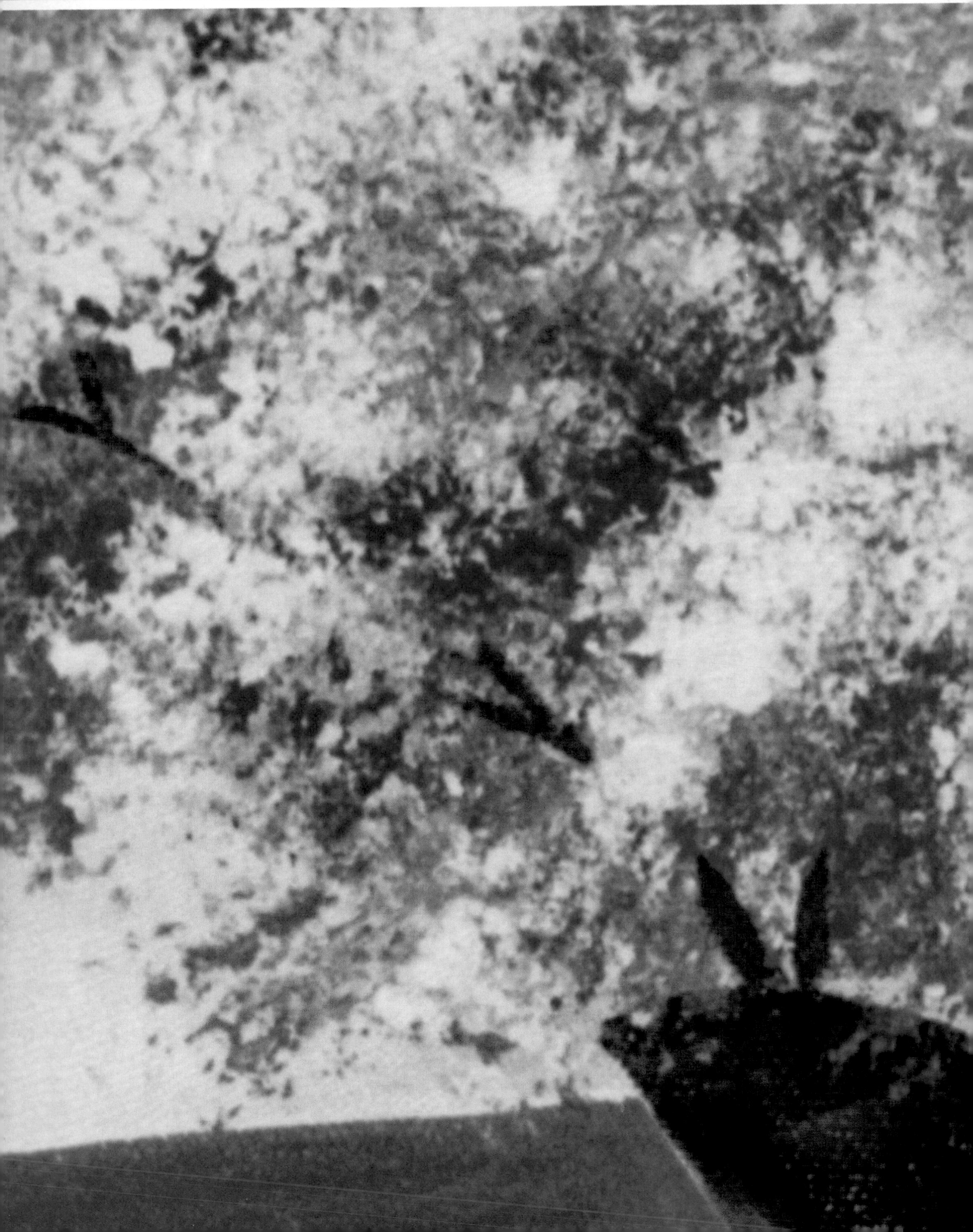

P·A·I·N·T·I·N·G

Acrylics are a relatively new medium to the painting world. Having been available for only the past fifty years, they are known as "the paints that artists have been waiting for".

Versatile and flexible, these paints can emulate both oils and watercolors.

The project "Blue Chair and Lilacs" is an ideal example of acrylic painting. Follow the step-by-step instructions and see if you agree that these are paints worth waiting for.

Blue Chair and Lilacs

Acrylic paints are new to the world of painting, only about 50 years old. Oils have been around for centuries.

Most artists feel that acrylics are the ideal paints. They are known as the most versatile because by adding different mediums to the acrylics you can imitate both watercolor painting and oil painting.

One of the best things about acrylics is that they dry very quickly, so unlike oil painting, you don't have to wait to lay down the next layer until paint dries. Acrylics come in a very wide variety of colors. Another advantage of acrylics is that the canvas does not have to be primed.

There are certain techniques you will need to learn in order to create your own acrylic masterpiece!

1. Opaque technique - using the paint right out of the tube and mixing with a little water to produce a creamy consistency.

2. Transparent technique - mixing much more water into the paint to produce a wash which is transparent.

3. Scumbling - scrubbing motion that spreads a veil of color across the surface of the canvas.

4. Dry Brush - skimming the brush across the surface - the paint hits only the high points of the textured paper producing flecks of color where the brush touches.

You will probably use a combination of these techniques in your paintings as you progress.

Materials needed to get started:

Paint
Basic beginner assortment: Ultramarine, Phthalo Blue, Cadmium Red, Naphthol Crimson, Cadmium Yellow, Yellow Ochre, Phthalo Green, Chromium Oxide Green, Burnt Umber, Mars Black, Titanium White

Brushes
Use synthetic brushes at first. A nice beginning assortment would include:
1" and 1/2" flat bristle brushes
1" and 1/2" soft hair brush
#6 and #10 round soft hair
#6 and #8 flat

Painting Surface
Illustration board (smooth surface)
Watercolor paper
Canvas

Palette
Enamel tray
Plastic or paper palettes

Other supplies
Paint box
Palette knife (for mixing color)
Sharp knife (to cut paper)
Paper towels
Sponge
Pencil
Kneaded eraser
3 jars (one for brushes, one to clean brushes, one for diluting paints)

Painting mediums
You can create many varied looks, using acrylic paints and adding different mediums:

Retardants - Slows down the drying time. Use 20% retardant to paint.

Gels - increases the translucency without altering the consistency

Heavy Gel - thickens paint, increases transparency, helps to give appearance of oil paints

Opaque Gel - bulks out paint, doesn't affect color. Helps you to do impasto work.

Gloss - Increases translucency. Gives a glossy finish. Can be used as a varnish when painting is finished.

Matte - Improves the flow of the paint and gives a matte finish. Do not use as a varnish.

Extender - Adds thickness to paint so you can create different textures.

Modeling Paste - thickens paints in order to get thicker, 3-dimensional textures.

Painting from a photograph is a good way to start out and to practice techniques. It's easier to see tonal values in a photograph.

Tip- To keep a palette of paint moist overnight (or longer) cover with plastic wrap and place in freezer.

The Project

Palette
Burnt Umber
Ultramarine
Yellow Oxide
Phthalo Green
Dioxide Purple
Black
White
Brushes -
#3 bristle flat
1" soft hair flat
#10 (1/4") round soft hair
#6 (1/8" wide) round soft hair
#6 (1/4") flat
#8 Flat
Other supplies -
Sea sponge
16" x 20" canvas

1. Sketch the composition on the canvas with pencil or a #3 round brush with Burnt Umber thinned with water.

2. Start with the background using a #3 bristle flat brush. Loosely brush in the shaded areas in back of the chair. The very light areas are a mixture of White with a very little Yellow Oxide, Burnt Umber and a tiny bit of Green. The Medium Gray areas are a mixture of Black, White, Burnt Umber and Yellow Oxide. The dark areas are Burnt Umber an Black. The baseboard under the chair is painted with a mixture of White, Yellow Oxide, and Burnt Umber. (Notice that this has been darkened along with the rest of the area under the chair in Step #4.

Tip- On your palette, mix up a "color pool". With each of the main color you are using - mix a dark, medium and light shade, then as you paint you'll have these handy and not have to stop and mix them.

Paint in the blue chair. This is a mixture of
Ultramarine, Dioxide Purple and White. Add a little
black to shade. Add White to the mixture for
highlighted areas. Notice where the highlighted areas
are...at the right front of the chair seat, the top of the
chair back and the top corners of the ladder backs.
Also notice the highlights on the legs and rungs, under
the chair.

Brush the Light Blue on the chair seat with the brush
strokes going from the front to the back with most of
the lightest color at the front.

Shade the chair by adding Black to the blue mixture.
Notice where the shaded areas are: The left edge of
the seat, the back leg, the rungs under the seat. Now
you can start adding some of the details to the chair.
Using a small brush, add the thin white highlights on
the back of the chair. Using the same brush, with a
mixture of the Blue and Black, add the dark areas
where the ladder backs meet the edge of the chair.
Also, where the legs meet the seat.

Paint the whole pitcher with Burnt Umber, shade with
Black. Brush the highlights on with a watery mixture
of Burnt Umber, White and Yellow Oxide. Use a large
brush for the wide areas, smaller for the small areas.
Notice highlights on the handle and around the base.

4. The lilacs: put three values of Dioxazine Purple on
your palette - light, medium, dark and white. Using a
sea sponge, dip it in the medium purple first and dab
it onto the canvas, blocking out your flower area.
Paint in the stems with Dark Green. Squint your eyes
and notice where the dark areas are on the painting.
Dab the dark purple in these areas.

Next dab in the light areas and lastly dab in white in
the lightest areas. Put some Green (mixed with White
on your palette and dab the sea sponge in it - add to
the flowers.

If you've enjoyed painting this and want to continue
with acrylics, set up your own still life. Shine a light
on it to exaggerate the shadows and highlights.

Learn as much as you can from a book about
perspective and composition. Study the paintings of
the old masters. You might also want to register for a
class at your community college.

Enlarge 200%

Two examples of different painting techniques from some of the same still life elements...Kathy's painting has beautifully expressive brush strokes which suggest the subject rather than render it. Barbara's painting is done in a more realistic and detailed manner which captures the reflections in the tin containers.

Barbara Finwall

Kathy Morgan

Another painting by Kathy Morgan, done with very painterly brush strokes, seems to glow from within.

S·O·U·R·C·E·S

Aleene's / Duncan Ent.
5673 E. Shields Ave.
Fresno, Ca 93727
Stencils

American Traditional Stencils
442 First Newhampshire Tpke
Northwood, NH 03261
Stencils

Arty's
Sinoart, Inc,.
Box 1650
Windsor, Ca 95492
Silk Painting Kits

Back Street
3905 Steve Reynolds Blvd.
Norcross, Ga 30093
Paint, Faux Finish Kits,
Chunky Stamps, Stencils

Beacon/Signature
P.O. Box 427
Wyckoff, NJ 07480
Glass Plates

Benjamin Moore
51 Chestnut Ridge Rd.
Montvale, NJ 07645
Paint

Decorator & Craft Corp.
428 S. Zelta
Wichita, Ks 67207
Papier-Mache Boxes

Delta Technical Coatings
2550 Pellissier Pl.
Whittier, Ca 90601
Paint, Stencils

Dressler Stencil Co.
253 SW 41st St.
Renton, Wa 98055
Stencils

The Glidden Company
925 Euclid Ave.
Cleveland, Oh 44115
Paint

Ikea
185 Discovery
Colmar, Pa 18915
1-800-434 4532 (for catalog)
Furniture Pieces

Kraft Klub
12325 Mills Ave. #23
Chino, Ca 91710
Papier-Mache and rusted
tin items

Loew Cornell
563 Chestnut Ave.
Teaneck, NJ 07666
Brushes

Mangelsen's
8200 J Street
Omaha, Ne 68127
Glass items

MPR Associates
529 Townsend Ave.
High Point, NC 27263
Paper Lace

C.M. Offray & Sons
360 Rt. 24
Chester, NJ 07930
Ribbon

A Place in the Garden
9121 Valley View
Cypress, Ca 90630
Wood pieces

Plaid Ent.
1649 International Ct.
Norcross, Ga 30093
Paint, glazes, Faux Finish kits,
Stencils, Tools

Rust-Oleum
American Accents
11 Hawthorn Parkway
Vernon Hills, Il 60061
Paint

Syndicate Sales
2025 N. Wabash St.
Kokomo, In 46903-0756
Glass pieces

Tara Materials, Inc.
322 Industrial Park Dr
Lawrenceville, Ga 30246
Floor Cloths

Walnut Hollow
1409 State St. Rd. 23
Dodgeville, Wi 53533
Wood pieces

Winni Millers' Dry It Board
P.O. Box 3130
Fallbrook, Ca 92028
Dry It Board

Wooden Hen
7389 State, Rt. 45
Lisbon, Oh 44432
Wood pieces

The authors wish to thank the following companies for their kind permission to reproduce their photographs in this book:
Benjamin Moore 4, 5, 10, 11; Glidden Paints 6 and 7; Plaid Enterprises 21-27, 78-81;
Dressler Stencil Co. 32-33, 43; American Accents 50-53, 54 57.